Search Your Company

Your Customers Will!

By

Jason Myers

Table of Contents

Foreword

Jason has put together a great overview of what it takes for a commercial contractor to be found online. His belief is that ProView is a critical part of not only finding enough jobs in the marketplace but also more critically finding the jobs that are the best fit for you and the client to ensure a successful and profitable project for all parties.

He asked me to give you a brief overview of ProView and its parent company The Blue Book. The Blue Book has been a valued resource for the construction industry for over 100 years. Our system is invaluable for assisting contractors and subcontractors to find appropriate projects.

We realized very early on that information was moving online rapidly, so over 15 years ago we made the commitment to become an industry leader online, just as we have been an industry leader for over 100 years in print.

As we moved information online we quickly realized that there were some major issues facing commercial contractors in the online world. The biggest challenge we found was in trying to differentiate commercial construction and the people that are experts in it from all the noise that was being created online by the residential construction industry. Whether it was paid advertising or search engine results, when you searched online there was very little to differentiate a commercial specialist from all the residential contractors vying for attention. For example, when you searched for a company to install a deck you are much more likely to find residential builders that specialized in building wood decks on the back of your home then you were to find any commercial contractors that built steel decks on your building.

It was obvious that it was very important for us to find ways to get the right information in front of the right users to help ensure our clients success. And if you pardon my bias, I believe we've done a pretty good job of doing just that. Our massive investments and ongoing investments in both time and money have made our website one of the top ranking sites in the commercial construction area and according to the world ranking website Alexa we have a ranking of 11,533, which is even more impressive when you realize that that ranking is out of over 800 million websites on the Internet. And even more importantly, we have monthly visits by over 400,000 unique users. These are the actual decision-makers - the people that make the buying and hiring decisions in the commercial construction industry. With over 1.5 million page views each month we have become the "go to" source for information in the commercial construction industry.

Once we became one of the dominant information providers online, publishing over 300,000 projects each year, it put us in a position to see that not only were people using project information sites like ours but more importantly, we realized that they were using the Internet as a vital part of their process for qualifying contractors during the invitation to bid process. Whether it was a new customer or a previous customer, the term "Google it" had become a vital part of their due diligence process.

We created a system that we called ProView that has developed into the nucleus of every successful commercial contractor's online marketing program. We developed the ProView systems to ensure that decision-makers could find the critical information that they needed. Whether coming to our ProView site at the beginning of their project to search for viable candidates, or using our information to check out an existing vendor, we made sure that they were able to easily find the exact information they needed, when they needed it, to make qualified decisions. That's really the critical piece of this, developing solutions to help people become more productive when they're going through the buying and hiring process.

Even though there are many companies that provide good solid project information, we are the only ones who also provide actual contractor information, the "who's who" of the commercial construction industry. No other companies combine both project and contractor information in one place. This allows you to triangulate who the players are, what they are doing, and what projects are a good fit for your business. We are the dominant player in this industry.

Even with all of the investments and successes we've had online we haven't forgotten one of the key ingredients to our success over the last hundred years.

This industry is and will always be, in our opinion, relationship based, so one of the key differentiators that we have in this company is our feet on the street. We have an army of close to 300 people in the field every day, working directly face-to-face with architects, owners, general contractors and subcontractors. As more businesses try to morph into the Internet only business, that's typically what they attempt to take away. Their goal is to deal exclusively online.

But we still recognize that this industry is relationship based and will continue to make that a priority. Having said that, we will continue to take advantage of all the current technology for helping us grow the network to provide more value for our customers and to ensure that we constantly apply state of the industry marketing techniques, like those Jason has outlined throughout this book.

We will continue to stay at the leading edge for information and delivery systems in our industry. Our goal for the next hundred years is the same as it's been for the last hundred - to do everything possible to ensure that our clients have the information that they need to operate their company successfully.

Richard Johnson

President - The Blue Book

www.thebluebook.com

Introduction

If you have been sitting on the fence trying to figure out how you can use marketing to drive more leads into your construction business, then this the right book for you. Within these pages are search engine marketing, social media marketing and offline marketing strategies and tactics proven to grow businesses. Massive success is closer now than its ever been.

In fact, the current state of the economy is the perfect storm for business owners who are nimble and willing to ride the wave. However, taking advantage of opportunity comes with one requirement: you must take action *now*.

No more stalling, no more procrastination, no more day-dreaming about what you should do. No longer can you sit on the fence, waiting and hoping for a magic bullet to solve all your marketing problems. The truth is that you are guaranteed to continue struggling if you are sitting back and hoping for that magic bullet.

What you hold in your hands is the ultimate step-by-step blueprint to guide you through the danger-riddled, but rewarding journey of setting up marketing systems that will grow your business *today*. Most of these will work for virtually any business and although a few of them may not be a perfect fit for construction companies, I include them to provoke thought.

In this book I have compiled dozens of marketing strategies that successful business owners are using right now to consistently break sales and revenue records month after month. None of these strategies are untested theoretical ideas that haven't seen the light of day. Each marketing strategy and system has been painstakingly applied and leveraged to produce consistent results in every type of business imaginable.

Included is information you will want to have in order to effectively market your business, but more importantly, I have included the information that you will NEED to know to avoid getting ripped off, losing your sanity or giving up on gowing through marketing.

The book you hold in the palm of your hand is unique in four major ways. This book will:

1. Prepare you to become an expert at getting leads into your business by empowering you with the exact information you need to know to market your business. Nothing has been left out.
2. Break down all the vital parts of writing marketing messages that get leads and drive growth into your business. It is not just a few scattered pages about marketing online, ads, training staff and so on. This book gives you a birds-eye view and then swoops down for an in-the-trenches inspection of each piece of the marketing formula.
3. Be used as your personal guide to marketing your business in your local area. There are plenty of books about running a business or marketing, but this is the first book to extensively focus on marketing your business locally.
4. Hand you the keys to unlock every piece of knowledge and resource that you will need to market your business successfully.

After reading this one-of-a-kind business marketing blueprint you will know:

1. How to use a simple piece of paper and a pencil to create marketing pieces that bring clients to your business within five to ten days.
2. The easy way to setup marketing systems that run on autopilot and allow you to increase your profits by more than you have ever dreamed would be possible.

3. The security of success. You'll finally be confident in yourself because you have the knowledge, tools and resources to grow your sales, profits and personal income.

By investing in this book you have now opened the door to an entire library of information about marketing your business that will serve as encouragement and yes, even sometimes an occasional slap on the wrist.

Additionally, I have made a special marketing toolset available only to you as a thank you for investing in this book. To download the toolset, simply go to: **http://searchyourcompany.com.**

Jason Myers

P.S. While I cover a lot of marketing topics in this book, there are simply too many to cover every one of them. Some of the proven topics not covered include: email drip marketing, marketing automation and behavior based targeting and retargeting. To learn more about these topics, connect with me at **http://www.searchyourcompany.com.**

Chapter 1

David versus Goliath

"You have to learn the rules of the game and then you have to play better than anyone else" ~ Albert Einstein

In today's ever-changing search engine landscape, the commercial contractor has the exceptionally difficult job of standing out in a sea of consumer-oriented businesses with huge advertising and search engine optimzation (SEO) budgets.

Do you want to advertise your commercial contracting business online? Great, you'll be competing with every residential contractor out there. This drives web Pay Per Click (PPC) or Pay Per Impression (CPM) based advertising on Google and other platforms up to exorbitant levels.

Furthermore, click quality is diluted by buyers (clickers) who, more often than not, are looking for a residential solution. Enter the organic SEO tactic. A wise commercial contractor would expend resources to strengthen the performance in the organic SEO of specific commercial/industrial contracting phrases. This process of SEO optimization is neither fast, nor is it a one-time project. In fact, consistent focus and constant re-education are required to keep up with search engine algorithm (methodology) changes, which occur at least each quarter.

The question is, what can a contractor do to maintain a web presence that drives inquiries?

By the Numbers

The lion's share of traffic to websites is driven by Google. Google is the 800-pound gorilla. To put the power of Google into perspective, one must dive into the data. Some of the most compelling statistics clearly show that Google is the most important topic for website owners looking to leverage its search results and the traffic it can deliver.

Here are some notable facts:
- Nearly 25% of all internet traffic comes from Google
- Google commands about 40% of all online advertising spend
- About 60% of all internet enabled devices connect to Google on a daily basis
- Half of a website's traffic will typically come from search results

The bottom line in the search engine war is that Google is on top.

SEO Reality vs. Fiction

One area of concern that has largely been blown out of proportion by SEO practitioners is the fear of "duplicate content." Google describes this as having "substantive blocks of content within or across domains that either completely match other content or are appreciably similar."

From a purely academic perspective, if you take large paragraphs and paste them onto multiple pages on your site or on to other sites, there is a chance that Google will either remove the duplicate pages or rank one of the pages ahead of the others. In some cases, the page that ranks well may not be the one that you want to be ranked higher. The duplicate content threshold is more severe within a given website than across multiple domains.

Google has been working to crack down on sites that scrape/copy content from one site and repurpose it onto others in order to drive traffic, users, and revenue for them. This is not to be confused with high-trust sites that provide value- added exposure to the content.

When a business is listed on a high-trust website, that listing in and of itself is not duplicate content. In fact, the typical contractor website gets less than 100 unique visitors per month and has very little off-page SEO. Contrast this with niche websites like TheBlueBook.com, where the content is highly relevant to those searching for contractor-related information. This "focus" creates clarity and trust in the eyes of Google. These "trusted" sites have an actual trust rank with Google that any independent contractor website is hard pressed to duplicate. A fun exercise is to compare a site like TheBlueBook.com to your website or the website of a competitor using one of the online tools to see which one is trusted more. Of course, higher trust helps provide higher search engine results. Access my free tool at SearchYourCompany.com

It's A Zoo Out There!

It appears that animals are on the loose, in terms of search engine updates. Every time we turn around, another animal has emerged, creating havoc for website owners. These animalistic changes are meant to improve the search experience for real users. This is a bit of a shell game for website owners and SEO geeks, where Google will adjust its formula to increase or decrease the weighting of certain factors used to determine the ranking of a web page in the search engine results page (SERP). Why do they do this? Because everyone is trying to improve website rankings by leveraging the on-page and off-page SEO methods. When one method is overused, creating a poor result set, mighty Google will adjust the weighting to rebalance the results.

Is Google picking on you - the "little" guy? Far from it. They are picking on everyone, from Ebay to the Wall Street Journal. They will even create impacts to website businesses that they (Google) themselves own!

There seem to be three camps when it comes to focus on SEO: the avoider, the dabbler, and the committed. Regardless of which camp you currently belong to, you must realize that changes to search engines are perpetual and that with each change comes new adjustments that increase or decrease the impact to anything you may have done to site's performance. To illustrate this, check the revision oogle algorithm at SearchYourCompany.com

ever-changing search engine landscape, the commercial contractor has an especially difficult job: stand out in a sea of consumer-oriented businesses with huge advertising and SEO budgets.

The Four-Factor Formula to Successful On-Page SEO

The most important factor for a site is the on-page (within the site) optimization. Off-page SEO is mostly about creating votes of confidence and relevance from third-party sites, and is not as important in today's search engine landscape. There are four distinct on-page factors in a successfully executed SEO-friendly website:

Platform + Architecture + Curation + Content = On-Page SEO

Let's start with *Platform*. It must be fast. Page load times represent a major factor in the search engine indexing robot (Bot) being able to fully index the site. Take a look at your site using Google Webmaster Tools at SearchYourCompany.com. It'll show you the latency or speed issues that may be affecting your site each time the Bot crawls it.

Most contractor websites use GoDaddy free or low-cost shared hosting or something comparable. This exposes the site to traffic spikes or systemic risks on any number of the hundreds or thousands of sites hosted on that single server. Want to know how many websites are hosted on your shared server?

Check out **www.SearchYourCompany.com** and perform a reverse IP lookup.

There are three issues that might result from seemingly "affordable" shared hosting:

1. Latency: Speed issues (i.e., slow page load times) caused byneighbors hogging all of the server processing power and bandwidth.
2. Guilt by association: If there are spammers, undubious characters or poor actors on the same server, the search engine can penalize your site.
3. Malicious attacks: These can result in hidden malicious code on sites that phish or otherwise compromise the visitor by stealing data and other nefarious activities. One unsecure site on the server can jeopardize the entire network of neighbor sites on the server. This is much like an outbreak of the flu in a family because of contamination and close proximity. Thousands of sites in a two-square-foot box is the epitome of close quarters.

Architecture is how the site is designed from a Bot perspective. Specifically, can the Bot crawl the site's navigation and content in a logical fashion? Is the structure of the site logical for a human and does it allow for proper comprehension?

Curation is the portion where the business owner or website person steps in and adds new content to the website on a regular basis. However, this is not to be confused with only text-content. Typically, during this process is when many on-page SEO mistakes are born. For example, while adding pictures of a project, the curator may skip the meta-information on the image (Alt tag). This creates an issue for the Bot to determine what the image represents, and this in turn affects the page that the image appears on by reducing the evidence to the Bot as to what the page is about. In another common scenario, the curator is adding content to a post or page in a content management system (CMS), and forgets to use proper title, description, keywords, and other meta-information to help the search engine. The result is poor latent semantic index[ing] (LSI). The end result is that the Bot needs to try harder to determine what the page/site is about. One thing is for sure, when the Bot is required to work harder, it simply moves on and the website is not fully represented.

Content is something that has become more and more talked about in terms of SEO and its importance. It makes sense that the Bot is trying to determine what the site is about - similar to how a human would. Many ill-advised webmasters and SEO geeks will try to game the system. However, the reality is that good information is looked upon favorably. Information that is poor, stale, or poorly written will be penalized in terms of search engine ranking for relevant keywords and key phrases.

The key is to realize that evolving content is fresh and that it gives the Bot something new to chew on. In recent years, Bots have favored fresh, almost up-to-the-minute information. The fact is that with billions of web pages, freshness is better than stagnation.

The Mysterious Hunt for Off-Page SEO

The most effort and expense for SEO activity is expended on off-page optimization. This effort is also the target of major search engine algorithm updates. Why? Because it has been the most "gamed" by amateurs and pros alike. The idea behind off-page SEO is to create references, votes of confidence, and relevance from third-party sites.

This is not as important in today's search engine landscape as it once was. Make no mistake, however, it still matters. Not every vote is equal. For example: If your site had a link on Wikipedia, that link would be a high-quality, high-trust inbound link. The result would be a positive effect on your website. The trust rank and page rank are key factors in weighting the impact of an inbound link on your website. The key takeaway here is that you should have a solid handful of high-trust, high-quality inbound links.

One of the ways to make sure your construction company gets a solid vote of confidence, or a boost by association, is to have your ProView on TheBlueBoook.com linking to your website. To be found using a variety of search phrases, it is recommended to link from your website to your ProView, and your ProView will be a high-trust, high-quality link pointing back to your website. Think of this as partnering for success.

Now, some SEO service providers will advise against this reciprocal linking methodology. This is one of the examples of over-generalization causing confusion. To be clear, reciprocal linking is not inherently bad, but who you do it with can be bad.

One-way linking from or to similar content is best. For reciprocal linking, follow this rule of thumb:

- Link with sites you trust
- Link with sites in your industry
- Natural linking with/to similar content is best
- Don't use link exchanges/farms/link-building services

The final thought on the off-page SEO topic is to avoid large, artificial work efforts to add or remove inbound links. There are SEO firms that prey on misinformation and over-generalization, making an entire cottage industry out of these add/remove link efforts. Be natural, with trustworthy sites, and enjoy natural results.

www.SearchYourCompany.com

Chapter 2

It's Not Who You Know, It's Who Knows You

In Offline Marketing, the term Local Marketing can generally refer to "any non-internet marketing techniques a localized business, in any industry, uses to market itself to the area it operates in."

In Online Marketing, Local Marketing generally refers to "any online marketing techniques that a local business, in any industry, uses to market itself online to the area it operates in."

Local marketing is mostly used by small businesses like stores, restaurants and outlets, but franchise businesses and contractors also use local marketing to promote themselves around their specific location.

A local company uses specific marketing strategies to engage new and potential customers related to their specific community. Transferring that same marketing activity to the online marketing world may bring some outstanding results that can easily surpass those offline marketing activities.

A huge percentage of potential clients search online to discover and research your compnay, before they ever reach out.

Local Marketing provides you with the ability to understand your customer's behaviors and purchasing habits a lot more, because you can know more about your customers online than you can know just by their coming into your store.

You can use online channels like your website, mobile applications, social media, local search and emails to attract local customers, which can offer more power for influencing your prosepects and customers.

There are four key elements that you need to be aware of when immersing your Local Business into the Local Marketing world:

1. Segmentation: defines how one group of customers is distinguished from another group of customers. It also refers to "who" you are going to target.
2. Media: determines "how" you will deliver your message. It shows what type of media you are using to communicate with your audience like website, mobile applications, social media, local search, emails, etc.
3. Messaging: defines "what" you are communicating. These messages are directed to the local population, rather than the mass market. It establishes what you should say to your audiences and in which manner you should convey those messages to turn your audience into customers.
4. Measurement: is essential for evaluating your marketing efforts and measuring your results. Positive results can show you how good you are at satisfying the needs of your customers.

Local marketing is an endless process. Most businesses make the mistake of treating marketing as a one-time campaign or event. If you have the correct approach and do it right, it will always give you the highest return of your marketing investment.

Using Local Marketing On The Web

In the online marketing world you can use online marketing strategies to do local marketing so you can build your brand awareness in your area.

It is all about how you can reach, know and interact with your audience as much as you can. Here are a few online media channels normally used to target local audiences:

- Local Website: local customers normally get excited when their favorite store has a website showing their products and services. It's easier for a customer to plan with the use of a webpage where is he or she going to buy stuff before going there.

  Having a very informative and constantly updated website will be a great help to your target audience. The majority of people feel too lazy to call sometimes, so it's just easier and more fun for them to go online and browse a website.

- Local Social Media: people hang out a lot more on social media networks than on a website, and that's where you should establish your presence as well. I have no words to explain how much time, money and effort social media has invested on behalf of local businesses.

  The number of followers, likes, shares, reviews, comments, retweets and any other social action shows the interest of your audience in your products. Responding and engaging other social media users is a good way to show that you care about your audience and business.

- Local Search: is your website listed by your location and the local market it serves? Are the keywords and descriptions you used for the search engines used by those people who are searching for a business like yours in a specific area, for example 'Electrician in Boston' and 'Plumber in Miami'?

  It is amazing the fact that you can target your audience directly by positioning your local business in front of them with the use of search engines. It has been proven that ranking at the top of the search engines for local terms is easy.

  And the greatest thing is that just a few of your local competitors know about it, which puts you in a unique position to "Steal" their customers by using the internet.

- Local Mobile: the time has come when every single thing created to be used on a desktop computer has to be optimized for mobile devices. If you don't go mobile optimized with your webiste, you will certainly be missing out on a great deal of customers.

- Local Lead Generation: I have seen how important and trusted Cost per Action (CPA) websites pay $10 to $200 for every new lead generated on behalf of a business. Having your local customers in a contact list is one of the greatest thing you will ever do on behalf of the ongoing success of your business. List Building is the greatest internet marketing strategy ever, and you can even do it locally.

The Benefits of Local Marketing

Credibility

Having your business' local presence everywhere on the web will increase your business' authenticity on the web.

If you place your business on the web with images, physical address and valuable information about your products and services, viewers will rely on your local listings more than other traditional listings.

According to an NDA Group report, about 57% of online customers [research] online, but they buy offline.

Stronger Access to Local Market

It's so easy to take advantage of local marketing just by having a direct connection with your customers and community. This will maximize the chance to gain additional and future opportunities.

You can also refer the services of other local businesses that offer complementary services. In turn, they will come back to you with extra added benefits, because other local businesses in your communities will refer you to their customers.

Brand Loyalty

A really high level of customer service and the creation of top quality products will help you to build your brand in your local community. Make sure to offer quality and provide the best services to your customers.

You can also use social media for communication and engagement with your customers. Social media can be the best way to gather brand loyalty for your local business if you update it on a regular basis.

Accessibility for Mobile Searchers

If your website is registered in local directories and has a mobile optimized layout, your viewers can easily find and navigate it. This will add an extra advantage over your competition.

Millions, if not all, mobile devices have applications which help the customer find any business near them. These applications will help you get a large amount of potential.

Easy to Implement
Complexity is your enemy, when it comes to marketing. One of the keys on the web is to make it as easy as possible for the user.

The same can be said about Local Marketing. You will be amazed how much time, money and effort important companies are spending to create the greatest local marketing tools ever.

Targeting and Personalization
You will get extremely targeted mobile searchers for your business because you will know who the prospects are, where they come from and what they like.

With many advertising platforms you can target ads based on their demographic profile like age, gender, buying habits, geographic location, income level, occupation, hobbies and interests. You can do almost anything on the web.

Increase Revenue

How much do you usually spend on local offline marketing activities around your local business area? How much do spend online? How muhc do you think you should spend on mobile?

The principal idea of targeting a lot more of your local customers a lot faster on mobile is leading them to engage with your company more often.

Analytics

Analytics allow you to see who is looking for your business, when they last checked out your website and where they were online previously. That's something really hard to do offline.

These statistics will allow you to adjust your marketing plan accordingly. You can completely monitor your social media and website activities. All these things can have a positive effect on your productivity and return on investment.

Free Traffic

You will get a lot of free local-customer traffic to your website when you submit it to local directories.

Google states that 40% of mobile inquiries are related to local business searches. Several search engines also have local directories where you can submit your listing.

Channel Engagement

The less traffic your competitor's website gets, the more opportunity you have to engage those customers, promote your products and services in your community and increase your revenue streams.

As you know, local engagement is key to increasing your revenue. People will remember you because you are there constantly reminding them about your company.

Just the Facts

Here are some startling facts that will show you why you have to use Local Marketing to market your Business:

- 74% of Internet users perform local searches.
- More than 100 MILLION PEOPLE a month use Google Maps from mobile phones to find business information.
- 66% of American's use online local search, like Google local search to locate local businesses.
- 61% of local searches result in purchases.
- 54% of Americans have substituted the internet and local search for phone books.
- Microsoft has claimed that 53% of mobile searches on Bing are local in nature.
- 82% of local searches follow up offline via an in-store visit, phone call or purchase.
- Nearly ONE in TWO shoppers for local products and services are using their smartphones.
- Without a mobile presence, you are essentially neglecting or potentially insulting HALF of your target demographic.
- As much as 43% of Google Search traffic has local content.

Data like this makes it clear there is a lot of money to be made with Local Marketing. And while lots of people might be talking about it, very few can really teach you how to productively use Local Marketing on behalf of your business.

Chapter 3

Local Marketing Power Tools

Power Tool #1: Especially for Contractors – The Blue Book

There are a few things you can do to help promote your business more effectively. One of the most powerful tools you can leverage is the ProView from the Blue Book Building and Construction Network. ProView was designed, architected, built, and is constantly modified to keep up with all of the "animal" updates. Because the Blue Book website has a very high trust ranking and authority, your business, when listed with a ProView, is promoted to Google and the other search engines. ProView presents industry-specific, decision-maker focused information about your company. Some contractors have chosen to eliminate the hassle of maintaining a website by forwarding their website domain to their ProView. ProView provides a mobile-optimized trusted source of information about your company that can replace your website or supplement it by promoting you most effectively to the industry.

It is considered best practice to make sure that IF you maintain a website and a ProView, that you make sure to regularly update the ProView with the latest projects and other information. The ProView system is designed to be easier to update than your website. Whether you have a website and want to build a strong supporting site with ProView OR you want to replace/create your existing website utilizing the new ProView platform, the team at the Blue Book Building and Construction Network can help you at **http://www.thebluebook.com.**

Power Tool #2: SweetIQ

If your customers don't find you when they search, you might as well not exist, so SweetIQ is an all-in-one location based online marketing platform for local businesses, brands, and franchises.

A local and organic keyword tracker finds out the keywords that you can use to compete in local search. You can track your customers' activities on twitter and check-in on foursquare.

SweetIQ provides local competitor analysis for your business that monitors your local and organic keyword rankings on Google, Bing and Yahoo. It also tells you the online directories, social media profiles, blogs and websites that would help you to improve your local business rankings.

Local business listing management from SweetIQ discovers where your business is listed online, finds the gaps and gives you 100% local search coverage. It also identifies inaccuracies or inconsistencies and fixes them in a single click.

SweetIQ reviews, monitors, and listens where and what your customers are talking about regarding your business. Discover it at **www.searchyourcompany.com**.

Power Tool #3: MOZ Local

MOZ Local is designed for those who manage multiple local businesses. With MOZ Local you can easily manage your online listing. All you need to do is upload your business information with a click and it notifies you if any issues arise.

You can establish a consistent business listing in directories and popular websites with MOZ Local. MOZ Local emails you reminders to update and re-verify your information to establish correct and consistent listings.

The Category Research tool of MOZ Local helps you choose the right search engine categories. It also lists your local business with all five major U.S. data aggregators.

Power Tool #4: AllLocal

AllLocal was launched in 2008 to target individual needs of local markets. You need a unique approach to generate local traffic for your multi-location local business with a strong online reputation.

This problem is resolved by AllLocal. The AllLocal online platform decreases the required time to manage your business' local search presence.

It handles all the factors of local search like address validation, listing optimization, and google listings; it also tracks online reviews about your local business. It offers a customized location navigator, powerful bulk edit functionality and performance reporting.

AllLocal also provides online reports and the monitoring status of your listings that will help you to determine the retunrn on investment (ROI) that your local search listing will generate. Discover it at **www.searchyourcompany.com.**

Power Tool #5: Balihoo

Balihoo is the premier provider of local marketing automation with a cloud based platform that gets result for local markets. Balihoo is an automated marketing software for personalized local campaigns.

Balihoo drives relevant leads at local levels and makes sure that your local audience can find your product and services according to categories. Balihoo website templates are designed to drive local traffic.

It also helps national brands to get leads with online forms, focused call-to-action message and trackable calls. Its mobile websites are also optimized for search results and conversion because of built-in adaptive design with Balihoo.

Balihoo gives you easy to use templates, so just by adding your information you are all set with a great local marketing weapon in your hands. You will get real time analytics by individual location if you are running a multi-location based local marketing campaign. Discover it at **www.searchyourcompany.com.**

Power Tool #6: SproutLoud

You want to generate your brand awareness and drive sales to your local business from your local market, so SproutLoud can help you with customized local online marketing.

SproutLoud uses Local Search, Local PPC, Triggered Communications, Email Marketing, Direct Mail, Social Media, Mobile Sites, Review Monitoring and local media buying services to market your business locally.

Email marketing sends brand-approved emails to your targeted audience that will convert your audience into customers. It generates brand-approved paid search and ad campaigns with your business information so that your audiences will find you online and make their purchase immediately. Discover it at **www.searchyourcompany.com.**

Power Tool #7: SignPost

SignPost will feature your local business on every website and mobile application, including Google, Facebook, Yahoo, Yelp and many more.

SignPost is the simplest and most effective way to get found by your local customers. It will automatically update information on directories and social media sites to make you stand out from the crowd.

SignPost automatically advertises your local business to your new customers and targeted audiences. It will turn your local online advertising into real revenue by promoting your special deals.

You can engage your customer with social media channels and email marketing. You can also remarket to your old and potential customers to get them back. Discover it at **www.searchyourcompany.com.**

Power Tool #8: RioSEO

If you are a local marketer or have multi-location businesses and want software to optimize your local search or website, you can go for RioSEO tools for SEO automation, Content marketing, local search, reporting and competitive analysis.

Local search business listing management increases accuracy of your local business listings and organic local search presence. You can easily manage conversions tools and data with local SEO optimized landing pages, which maximizes the user experience and provides you with the detailed analytics report according to location.

You can target your local market with local SEO; it will find your search engine presence in Organic Search and Local Map Listings. You can optimize your local business listings for consistency on Google+ Local, Yahoo Local and Bing Places.

Discover it at **www.searchyourcompany.com.**

Power Tool #9: Kenshoo

Kenshoo local is an extendable platform to manage local marketing campaigns for individual stores, dealers, agencies and other local business. Kenshoo's tailored functionality will allow you to successfully manage your local search, places and directories listings.

The on-boarding and campaign management uses profile wizard, Campaign Template, Cross-Profile Advanced Search and Radius Geo-targeting that launches new local online marketing campaigns with an easy-to-follow guide, helping you to access saved templates, keywords and ad copy for advertising in local markets and target your local audience within a specified distance.

Kenshoo local manages your bids and goals with tools that are designed to optimize and scale. It automatically rolls over your unused budget with pre-set rules and an optimized search program to drive more leads to meet your business needs.

Discover it at **www.searchyourcompany.com.**

Power Tool #10: ElementsLocal

You are running a multi-unit company or franchise and want to promote it locally then ElementsLocal will help you deliver the power of your brand to your local customers.

ElementsLocal generates more leads, broadcasts your brand awareness, and enhances the presence of your online marketing. It includes consistent monitoring and tweaking to establish satisfactory results.

It uses email marketing, social media marketing and local search to empower your business strategy.

ElementsLocal automatically submits your franchise locations to search engines and directories and allows franchisees to update certain content. It also shows mobile friendly websites to customers who are using mobile devices. Discover it at **www.searchyourcompany.com.**

Power Tool #11: LocalVox

LocalVox is a local and social media platform that helps you market your business online. With LocalVox you can promote your local business across a network of publishers, social media, mobile, search engine and on your website - and all these are as easy as using your email account. LocalVox saves you time with a single partner and provides solutions for local internet marketing. It drives better results for your local business with an all in one marketing platform.

Discover it at **www.searchyourcompany.com.**

Chapter 4

Existing Database:
Make Them Raving Fans

Building your own in-house database of leads, prospects and past customers is critical. Now let's talk about the most effective and profitable ways to follow up with your database of prospects and customers and get them to purchase from you time and time again.

Following up with your database or nurturing your leads consistently is your new philosophy that you must whole-heartedly adopt in your business to be successful. However, it's more than just sending sales messages.

Your goal is to own the space in your customer's mind for the products or services that you offer. Prospects and customers always forget about your business over time. No matter how great the connection at the time a lead contacts or visits your business, the longer you wait to follow up with them, the more they forget you.

That's why your mission is to build relationships with qualified prospects regardless of their timing to buy, with the goal of earning their business when they are ready to buy. You accomplish this by consistently presenting the prospect with a persuasive sales message or educational message that compels them to visit your business and buy. You want them to feel as if they MUST come to ONLY your business when they're ready to buy AND when they're looking for information prior to buying.

Profitable Relationships

Follow-up marketing, also known as lead nurturing, is all about building a relationship with a prospect. You just can't force someone to commit (to a purchase, in this case) — but you also cannot afford to lose those individuals because they're not ready to buy today.

Most leads will eventually be ready, but it is up to you to both provide them with relevant information and to be there when they are ready to make a buying decision. The truth is that up to 95 percent of qualified prospects that express interest each day are there to research and are not yet ready to make a buying decision, but as many as 70 percent of them will eventually buy from you — or your competitors.

Business Insurance

Building a list of past customers and prospects that you can market your business to "on-demand" is your insurance policy against the revenue roller coaster most business owners have to endure.

Many Commercial Contractors think that bid opportunities find them and all they have to do is be the lowest bidder to win. Winning is winning at each stage of the project and being top-of-mind for the next project – especially negotiated and/or design/build type work.

Your database should be filled with thousands of leads, prospects and past customers who you can email, call or mail an offer to any time that you choose to keep your business top-of-mind. Imagine the power of sending out an email, text, postcard or letter on Tuesday and being booked solid or flooded with customers for the next six months from that one marketing effort. That's powerful.

However, the reality is that most business owners do the opposite. They spend thousands of dollars each month trying to get the attention of a small percentage of people who may possibly be ready today, but do little to keep in contact with people.

Don't Be an Average Joe

When it comes to follow up marketing, your goal is to not be just the proverbial Average Joe Contractor. Don't spend thousands of dollars on advertising or sponsorships, then sit back wish and hope that those efforts are good enough to attract new customers to cover the costs of ad and make a little profit. That's a tragedy that's replayed over and over in businesses all across the country.

Successful Business Owners Know That the Money Is In the List

The long-term and sustainable profits are in having a list of happy past customers and prospects to consistently market your offers to. If a person calls/walks-in/emails/visits your website or steps into your business, then you simply **MUST** make a conscious effort get their contact info. If you fail to do that, you will likely lose that lead forever.

Most business owners:
- Look at ongoing marketing to their past customers and leads as an expense instead of an investment.
- They are not willing to take the time away from their business to create a multi-step campaign that runs consistently.
- Are so busy working in their business that they don't have time to work *on* their business and create systems that will generate a huge increase in profits.
- Don't know and refuse to learn how to write educational, entertaining and persuasive marketing sales messages.
- Get overwhelmed by the technology required to setup automated follow-up marketing systems.

Most Common Excuses

Unfortunately, many business owners know the benefits of follow-up marketing. However, they allow themselves to buy into the excuses that hold them back from getting the most lucrative type of customer back.

The most common excuses are:

27

- Can't afford to pay for marketing to their database.
- Don't have their customers or prospect's information.
- Even if they had their contact information, don't know what to say.
- Don't know how to contact the customers or leads.
- Already have one million things going on right now.
- Don't have someone to do this for them.
- It seems too complicated.
- Don't want to learn to use any more technology.

Secrets to Follow-Up Marketing Success

In this section, I want to share with you the most powerful secrets that will allow you to experience massive success when you setup and implement your follow up marketing strategies.

Follow Up Marketing Success Secret #1:

The first follow-up marketing success secret is to completely understand the buyers in your target market. You need to interview and survey your customers, as well as those that didn't buy from you, in order to define your ideal customer profile and to develop buyer personas. You should ask questions like:

- What are their pains? What are their desires?
- What is their purchase process?
- Why were they interested in your product or service in the first place?
- What were the major factors in their purchasing decision?
- What else do you they want from your company?

Follow Up Marketing Success Secret #2:

The second follow-up marketing success secret is pinpointing and knowing the buying stage cycles for your products and services. This is so important because in order to create a follow-up marketing and nurture campaign that works, you must consistently deliver timely and relevant information to your prospects. If the information is too late, too soon or not relevant, it won't work.

You need to know and fully understand those stages and what works best with each. All buyers go through these three buying stage cycles:

1. *Stage #1: Just Started Looking*
    To get these prospects to come and buy from you, you need to have things like: free whitepapers, free books, free guides & tip sheets, free eBooks, free checklists, free videos, free kits and any combination of the above.
2. Stage #2: *Already Looking, But Need More Information*
    You need to offer things like free webinars & teleseminars, case studies, free product or service sample, frequently asked questions sheet requests, product spec sheets, catalogs, etc.
3. *Stage #3: Ready To Buy Now*
    You want things like free trials, demos, free consultations, estimates or quotes, coupons.

Follow Up Marketing Success Secret #3

Analyzing your past marketing campaigns in order to determine how they contributed to revenue is often overlooked or impossible – if you don't design them with the end-goal in mind. You'll want to look at the percentage of responses to campaigns and determine how many leads moved through all stages, and the messages and content offered at each stage.

You should have a folder and a binder (physical or on a computer) with every ad, promotion and sale you've ever run and the results of each. Otherwise, how will you know what worked and how you can improve upon it? Reviewing the success (or failure) of your past marketing efforts is the foundation upon which you build your follow-up campaigns.

Follow Up Marketing Success Secret #4

Visually map out the purchase path for each of your core products and services. You should have a piece of paper where you've mapped out your follow-up marketing campaigns that essentially mirrors your actual buying process.

The key to mapping this out is to start out with the end goal in mind and create a roadmap that is specifically designed to get a prospect to that end goal.

Be sure to develop a roadmap that makes the most sense for your business and try to anticipate any roadblocks to implementing it and address them early. If the objective is to send six emails and make three phone calls over eight weeks, what happens if you don't get the intended response after you do that? You need to have a plan for that.

Follow Up Marketing Success Secret #5

Automate your entire follow-up campaigns as much as possible. You already have enough on your plate to worry about. You don't want to have to manually send every email, lick every envelope, print every postcard, etc. Your follow-up campaigns must be able to be 99% automated with little human interaction needed to deploy or maintain the campaigns.

An automated "welcome campaign" is a great place to get started. Set up automated communications to greet those who enter your database and start delivering educational information right away.

There are over ten follow-up marketing campaigns you can and should implement in your business right away. Setting up these campaigns sounds like a lot of work, although it really isn't, but the trade-off is so

HUGE for your profits bottom line.

Do the work once and profit from it for years.

Eleven Types of Follow-Up Marketing Campaigns

Follow-up Campaign #1: Promotional Offer

This type of follow-up campaign on its face may not seem to apply to contractors because it is used to generate an instant influx of sales and profits by making an irresistible offer to your database. The promotional offer follow-up campaign can be used for all contacts on your database list – non-buyers and past customers alike.

The most important part of this follow-up campaign is that it must be built around an enticing and irresistible offer. Do you offer remodeling or repairs? This may be for you. It can't just be your normal every day and ordinary prices and packages that you always offer. You must also put an expiration date on the promotional offer so that people are forced to make a decision within the timeline you choose.

Follow-up Campaign #2: Post Purchase

This type of follow up campaign is designed for buyers only. The first couple of steps in this campaign should always revolve around:
1. Thanking the buyer for their purchase.
2. Reinforcing the good decision they made to purchase from you.
3. Share best practices to get the most out of their recent purchase.

After you've done those three key things, you can get very creative with the remainder of the campaign and do things like:
- Upsell closely related products or services.
- Cross-sell different types of other products or services that may complement their purchase.

- Deepen the relationship by continuing to educate the buyer on their purchase and share additional great features about their purchase.

Follow-up Campaign #3: Competitor Comparison

This type of follow-up campaign works great for companies that are in intensely competitive industries. This campaign focuses on educating your database on all the reasons why you're better than your competition. It can and should include case studies, testimonials and real-world test results from happy clients.

In order to be most effective, you could choose to have each message you send to your database focus on one key element of your product or service that is superior to your competition. However, make sure that you don't make personal attacks against your competitor. Focus on the superiority of your product or service only.

Follow-up Campaign #4: Top of Mind

This type of follow-up campaign is designed to keep your business in a prospect or customers mind. This campaign can work well for any type of business, but it's a necessity for businesses that sell service contracts (e.g., HVAC) or long term solutions.

While the goal of this campaign is not necessarily to sell a customer a product or service in every message, the occasional promotional message should be included. This campaign should be heavily branded with your logo, colors and unique sales proposition so that it's easily and instantly recognized as coming from your company.

Follow-up Campaign #5: Re-Engagement

This follow-up campaign is all about getting your past customers and prospects to interact with your company in some way. It could be through purchasing, but it should be through any number of ways like:

- — Requesting a catalog
- — Responding to an email
- — Calling into your office for more information
- — Visiting a website
- — Watching a video

The re-engagement campaign is all about getting past customers or prospects that showed interest previously to take another action to reconnect with your business in some way.

Follow-up Campaign #6: Renewal

This follow-up campaign is for customers who previously bought a series of products or ongoing service from you. The whole point of this campaign is to get them to once again sign up for the service that they previously cancelled, or that ran its course. It doesn't necessarily have to be a renewal of the service they've previously purchased. It can be a subscription to another service or series of products that you believe will help them. Just like when you're making a promotional offer, your success will be dependent on your ability to make an irresistible offer. If you primarily sell products without the option for ongoing services, now would be a great time to start offering subscriptions.

Follow-up Campaign #7: Topic-Based Campaign

This type of campaign is when you want to share information with your database on a specific topic. Of course, the topics you share should be closely related to products or services that you sell so that the contact can consume the information and then go on to purchase from you.

This type of campaign is great for building and deepening your relationship with your database as well. Also, while the first few messages in this campaign may be educational only, the final few should directly point the contact to your product or service that fits with the messages you've been sending to them.

Follow-up Campaign #8: Upsell

This type of follow-up campaign is designed to sell the customer additional products and services that complement their original purchase.

The power of this campaign is that it instantly increases your sales and profits without a huge increase in advertising expense.

In your upsell follow-up marketing campaign, you can offer:
- More of the same product or service they initially purchased.
- A larger quantity of the product or service they purchased.
- A bundle or package of additional services or products.
- Different products or services that you believe will help the buyers.

Follow-up Campaign #9: Onboarding

This campaign consists of follow-up messages that help a new customer get up and running with the product or service they purchased from you.

This campaign is an absolute necessity when the product or service you sell is complicated and requires a specific set of actions to maximize its benefits.

Many times you will see examples of onboarding follow-up campaigns when a customer purchased technology-dependent products or services. However, every business should have some form of onboarding to help their customers get the most value out of their purchase.

Follow-up Campaign #10: Training

This type of campaign allows you to focus on training your customers on the best way to use your products or services.

This campaign can also be a way for you to recommend some additional products and services that will also help the customer. This training can be provided in the form of reports, books, videos, and webinars or in your business in a physical location.

You can also provide training on all the ways other customers are using your products and services.

And don't be shy about promoting your other products and services during your trainings. That has proven to be an effective way to increase sales in a non-salesy way.

Follow-up Campaign #11: Blend of All Campaign Types

What you've probably already noticed is that you probably could use several or more of the follow-up campaigns in your business running at the same time.

That's normal and to be expected. In fact, it's common to add all of the campaigns at some point. For example, a post-purchase campaign can lead into an onboarding campaign which can flow into an upsell campaign which goes into a training campaign, etc. However, it's virtually impossible to do that without using automation technology. So, in the next section I'm going to talk about automating your systems.

Creating a multi-channel follow-up marketing campaign that is affordable, produces high quality leads, and runs on autopilot is the secret to practically all long-term successful companies. So I'm going to share with you the top six methods you can use to follow up with prospects leads or customers.

The Top Six Methods You Can Use To Follow Up With Prospects, Leads or Customers

Follow-Up Method # 1 Email

The first follow-up method is email. The majority of the country has an email address that they check weekly or daily, so it makes complete business sense to use email to follow up with your past customers and prospects.

Also, if you have a website, then you can likely send out emails for free. The good news is that you can sit down once and write the emails and then they can be scheduled weeks and months in advance and can be recycled and used again. So once you do the initial work you don't have to repeat it again. You just set it up.

Sending emails is a great way to build a relationship with your prospects and clients and its 100% trackable so you know who is opening and what's working. And best of all, it's virtually free to send out an email.

Follow-Up Method #2 Text Message.

The second follow-up method is text message or sms. This method has the highest open rate of all marketing communications. It's similar to when email first came out. The good news is that it can be used to generate instant sales and profits because of the high open rate. Just like email, it's 100% trackable, so you know who is opening and what's working. And it only costs one or two cents per text to send out.

Follow-Up Method #3: Recorded Message Voice Blasts

The third follow-up method is by pre-recording a message by phone and sending it to your list. Most businesses don't try to make the human connection series, so your real message will stand out if you are using a voice blast. Plus, it creates a stronger bond to your customers when they hear your voice. You can set this up and have a campaign going within five to ten minutes, and you can create your campaign online.

Follow-Up Method #4: Postcards

The fourth follow-up method is sending postcards. Postcards are a simple, inexpensive, but effective way to send your marketing message.

The receiver is practically guaranteed to see your marketing message when you send out a postcard.

The marketing message tends to be simpler and effective because the postcard is limited in size, and it's really affordable at typically 50+ cents per postcard.

Follow-Up Method #5 Letters/Newsletters or Sales letters

The fifth follow-up method is sending a newsletter or sales letter. Your newsletter or sales letter can range in length from one page to ten pages or more. The extra length allows you to tell your story in a compelling and persuasive way while generating sales. It also allows your customers to see behind the curtain of your business.

Follow-Up Method #6: Live Phone Calls

The sixth follow-up method is a live phone call. This can be a customer service follow up call/survey to see what other products and services your customers want from you.

People are desperate to know businesses care about their input and feedback. So, giving them a customer service or survey call makes them feel good. It's very affordable to do because you already have phone lines in your office. And it's easy and simple to actually implement, as it's just a phone call.

The Best Part Is...

- Five of these six follow-up marketing strategies can be automated and scheduled months in advance.
- More importantly, because they're automated and require very little human intervention, there's little chance for error.
- So few businesses are doing this that you will stand heads and shoulders above your competition in your marketplace.

- Plus, more importantly, you will have a proven marketing plan to generate sales consistently.
- And the ROI is HUGE. In many cases, you're spending less than $100 with the potential to generate tens of thousands of dollars in sales month after month.

Chapter 5

Referral Marketing Systems:
How to Generate Massive Sales and Profits by Getting Referrals from Your Customers and Local Businesses

Referrals are a gravy train that you should do everything in your power to consistently get. However, like most successful business building strategies, it takes real work and real changes, so many business owners avoid it like the plague.

To be honest with you, the large majority of business owners don't have a single system in place to generate referrals.

Missing the Boat

Getting referrals is great because you can get hundreds of people to visit your business at little to no additional cost. Plus, it's less expensive to generate referrals from existing customers than trying to get new customers. Referrals don't have to be convinced to come to your business because they've already been pre-sold on coming by other customers. When you create a referral marketing system, it's a strategic line that partners you with your past customers, but you also create an awesome customer environment that builds customer royalty.

Why Most Business Owners Are Not Worthy Of Receiving Referrals

- They have no real commitment to getting referrals.
- They are not doing anything unique or different that customers can recommend to other people.
- Being afraid of asking for referrals.
- There's too much focus on selfish reasons.
- They don't even remember to ask for referrals.

- Assuming that great service alone is enough.

The Golden Road

1. Level 1: Attracting people to your business
2. Level 2: Converting to loyal customers
3. Level 3: Taking Care of those First-Time customers once you get them in there
4. Level 4: Inspiring Iron-Clad Loyalty
5. Level 5: Customers start referring others back to you.

Customer Referral System

If you are running a good business then getting referrals from your past customers can be a goldmine for you. However, you always want your customer referral program to be a win. Therefore, you reward the customer who's referring someone, and you reward the referral for coming into your business.

Motivate Your Customers to Refer More

There are dozens of ways to motivate your customers to refer more prospects, so here's what you should do:

- You can host parties for local events or celebrations and offer free food to everyone who registers.
- You can host the fundraiser that benefits a local cause and require everyone to buy a raffle ticket and give you their contact information so that you can send them their prize.
- You may give your past customer loyalty rewards points for every first-time customer they refer.
- You can give away prizes like iPhones, amazon gift cards or even vacations to customers who refer certain amounts of first-time customers to your business.

How to Build Your Business Referral Generating System (aka. Strategic Marketing Alliances)

When two businesses work together to create a joint marketing campaign that benefits or drives customer growth to both businesses, it's called a Strategic Marketing Alliance. This can be done by mailing out letters of recommendations or endorsements to each other's customers and prospects. But, it can also be something as simple as handing out coupons or vouchers to their own customers which will then encourage the customer to visit the business of their strategic marketing partner. Regardless of the specific strategy used, the principle is that two different businesses are helping each other to become more successful.

The Bigfoot of Businesses

Strategic alliances are very effective ways of getting customers on a consistent basis, but this strategy does require you to step outside of your comfort zone in order to pull it off. That's why 99.9% of business owners don't even try to use this powerful business building strategy. However, don't dismiss it as being too hard, because it's so powerful that it can single-handedly transform your struggling business into a success. That's why it's one of the best ways for you to drive tons of your ideal customers to your business every day of the week.

Why Are Strategic Marketing Alliances So Powerful?

Strategic Marketing Alliances are one of the most powerful strategies you can get involved in because of seven reasons:

1. You will build a list of targeted customers and prospects that are most likely to dine at your business.
2. If done right, you will profit every time you form a strategic alliance, while also building your list.

3. Your partnerships are a good way to build great relationships with other business owners in your community that will pay off for years to come.

4. There's little to no advertising or additional marketing expense to get these customers to come into your business.

5. You can get access to a list of paying customers where someone else has already done the hard work.

6. It's easier to please these customers because you come highly recommended from a trusted source of theirs.

7. Using strategic alliances allows you to position yourself instantly as the best business because you're coming recommended from a trusted business.

The Strategic Alliance Mindset

When it comes to setting up Strategic Marketing Alliances, you need to make sure that your motives are pure. You need to approach this from a win-win perspective and not come across desperate or sleazy. You need to authentically come across as someone who is genuinely adding value to your strategic marketing partner. If you are blowing smoke, people can tell. However, if you're thrilled and enthusiastic, it will show and can have a positive impact on your potential partnership. That's why you need to come up with at least three to five things that partnering with you will help accomplish for your Strategic Marketing Alliance partner in their business.

Here are a few ideas as to what to look for in a Strategic Marketing Partner:

- You need a business that has a quality product or service that's a good fit for your customers.
- You need someone who believes in and practices consistent marketing and basic business building principles.

- You need someone who is trustworthy and operates in full integrity with everything they do.
- You need a business that you can feel proud of being associated with. Don't ever risk your reputation.
- You need a business partner who is willing to work, invest in and have a plan to make the alliance a success.

Endorsed Marketing Campaigns

An endorsed marketing campaign is when your strategic marketing partner creates some type of marketing piece where they directly recommend your business to their client database. This could be a direct mail campaign consisting of letters or postcards promoting your business with a list. Your strategic partner could also choose to send out an email blast to their database. In most cases, you would have a special offer for the customers that your strategic partner refers to you so that they know that you have a strategic alliance with that business.

Endorsements are powerful, and every strategic marketing alliance depends on the endorsement of its partners to be successful. For example, if your business partners with a caterer, then you need that caterer to speak good things about your business to their clients. Without the infamous "good word" being said about you, then your marketing alliance will fall flat and not work as planned.

That's why strategic alliances with good endorsements will always work better than any ad or marketing message that you send out to a list of people who don't know you. That's why endorsement-based strategic marketing alliances are often the most effective alliances.

While endorsement-based marketing alliances are the most effective

for your business, you must also acknowledge that they pose the most risk for your alliance partner as well. The best way to minimize this risk is to let your partner sample your business and service first and then clearly spell out what the irresistible offer for the alliance will be. Because if you screw up and drop the ball with the people your partner sends to you, then not only do you look bad, but the business that refers you also looks bad.

That's why it's always best to pay special attention to the customers that come to your business as a result of your alliance partnership. You may want to offer them special seating, parking or any number of special privileges so that the word will get back to your alliance partner that you treated them well.

Promotional Campaigns

An In-Business or on-premise Promotion campaign is when you and your strategic partner create marketing materials to be physically placed in both of your businesses to promote each other. This could be things like:

- Podium stands with tear-offs, images and advertising messages actively promoting your partner.
- Flyers placed in the business which advertise a coupon or voucher for customers.
- Banners that are placed in the business with an advertising message on the banner

A Co-Marketing campaign is an entire marketing campaign designed to promote the business of each strategic marketing partner. Things like newspaper, television, radio and social media ads with both companies advertising complementary products and services. This requires two businesses that are very much related to each other and valuable to the customer. This option also requires a high level of trust and tends to be the most expensive and complex option, But, the rewards of this option can be worth the risk if you do it well.

So before you say "I do" you must be able to provide a high-level quality experience for the leads your alliance partner or your referrals are sending to you. You should be prepared to create a true win-win partnership where you both get something good out of the deal. You need you make sure you have best deals around compared to your competitors.

You need to have your systems in place to track the leads or sales the alliance generates. You also need to have your tracking systems being as simple as possible as the customer needing to bring a special coupon or know a specific word or phrase may visit your business. You don't want it to be complicated,

So imagine you find five strategic marketing partner lists that each have a list of 1,000 people or businesses. By partnering with them, you've now just become the business of choice for 5,000 quality referrals from other businesses...with NO extra advertising cost!

On the other hand, the wrong Strategic Marketing Alliance can do massive damage to your business's reputation. That's why you must have systems in place to consistently deliver good products, service and experience.

Even after you've set up a strategic marketing alliance, you need to stay on top of things to make sure your partner doesn't drop the ball. You should find a reason to stop by, email or call them to update them and let them know you're available if they have any questions. You need to stay positive even if you do not see any results at first. Sometimes it takes a few weeks or even a few months for things to come together just right. Just be sure to get your partner to agree to a specific timeline for things to be completed to avoid any potential issues. If they start to lag, jump in and ask if there's anything you can do to help.

When you find a good alliance partner, you need to protect that relationship like you would protect your gold.

When good strategic marketing goes sour, it's, usually, because one or both of the partners are:

- Being cheap and not sharing costs evenly
- Being inflexible about dates, offers and compensation
- Being too casual about the partnership
- Making the other partner do too much work
- Being desperate
- Being greedy
- Guilty of not building a good relationship or rapport with each other

So, if you're not ready to handle the influx of customers, then don't do it. Also, you need to be prepared to give more than you're getting to make the strategic alliance attractive. And you need to have is several good ideas for a successful alliance with your partner and referrals.

To schedule a 30 minute consultant to see how I can help your business develop or execute its marketing plan, contact me at **www.searchyourcompany.com.**

Chapter 6

Customer Attraction Systems

In this chapter you'll discover the easiest and quickest way to motivate the right type of customers to choose your business. We don't want to fill your business with cheapskates. That's not the purpose of this book. We're going to talk about how to create a persuasive and compelling marketing message to your target audience.

I'm going to teach you how to make your business stand head and shoulders above your competitors and how you will always stick out in your customer's mind by giving you proven formulas you can use to make you the clear and obvious choice to your ideal customer.

You're also going to learn the real the truth about the secret way to get people to try your business the first time so that they can get hooked and give you an opportunity to get them as customers.

But first, can you answer this very important question...

Why should a person choose your business over any other and every other business that's available to them?

If you struggle to come up with an answer or can't answer that question, then chances are that your business is currently struggling now, and you may be on the verge of going out of business soon! This question is <u>that</u> important.

People won't consistently select your business if you don't have a compelling reason for them to do business with you. You may be able to scrape by with gimmies or referrals from buddies or waiting for walk-in traffic or maybe an ad you run every now and then, but you'll never get to high levels of success without a unique hook, something that speaks to your target prospects and motivates them to select your business.

The "thing" or "combination of things" that makes your business stand out in your customer's mind is called your Unique Sales Proposition (USP). A unique sales proposition can make all the difference for your business. It's the one thing that you have that you become known for or that people associate with your business.

It is also known as...
- Point of difference
- Unique Perceived Benefit
- Unique Selling Point
- Extra Value Proposition
- Competitive Advantage

But regardless of the name, it's the same thing... it's that thing that your business can do, or the experience that you can provide, that is your uniqueness. Not being able to distinguish yourself from your competitors is a curse that will haunt you for as long as your business is open until you address it.

How Effective Is Your USP?

A business with no unique sales proposition (USP) is always at the mercy of the market place, cheap customers or cutthroat suppliers. A business with no USP is also ripe for the picking for knockoffs, local competitors and big chain competition. After all, they do the same thing that everyone else does. As a contruction business, you are not immune and the clients can go elsewhere.

Therefore, you need to do something that makes your business unique and makes it stand out in your local marketplace. When you don't have a USP and your supplier prices or operating expenses go up, then your profits always go down because you don't give your customers any reason why they should pay you one penny more than they're paying you now.

An effective USP gives you the power in every area of your business. You get to pick the exact customer or customer you want. You get the power to set your own terms. You get the power to charge higher prices. You can dictate your terms to your suppliers because you deliver them so much business. You get to choose your busiest days or down time.

In short, your business is back under your control because you have this thing that can't be duplicated. You have this experience or ambiance that no one else can do the way that you do it, and so you can demand a premium for it.

A really good USP does more than just get you customers. It also sets the strategic direction for your business. It lets everyone know what to expect from your business. Your USP is not simply a marketing or advertising "thing." A compelling USP is more than a headline at the top of your ads. Your USP is the backbone of your business. A good USP is more valuable than any marketing gimmick, newspaper ad or flyer. In essence, it's your entire business.

There are many things that you need to make a really good USP that stands out on your customer's mind. Each advertisement must make a relevant, appealing offer to the customer or customer. This is the first step. It can't just be shallow words or purely advertising. The advertisement must tell the customer that if you come to business, you will get this specific result or benefit.

The offer you're making in your advertisement must be something that your competition cannot or does not or is not willing to offer. It must be unique in some way that makes it stand out in the minds of your target market. The offer must be so compelling that it can get people to get up off their couches right now and come to your business today. But, don't make a mistake of trying to compete on low price alone. As you build better USP's, and you get a proven track record for delivering on your USP, you should be raising your prices. That's the trade-off. It's what you strive to do. You strive to become unique.

There are two groups of USP's that you will have to create:
1. **USP Group #1:** This is your overall business USP that focuses on the general experience or expectations a customer should have when they reach your business.
2. **USP Group #2:** This is the USP you create for each specific ad, special, promotion, product or service that you offer.

You emphatically need both types of USP's for your business to stand out in the minds of your target market.

While a good USP can help your business consistently break sales records and grow profits, a bad USP can repel the exact customers you're trying to attract.

Here are some examples:
- "We've been in business for X amount of years." People really don't care about that anymore like they used to.
- "We have the lowest price for (whatever you sell)" That's a great way to go out of business in a few months.
- "We have every type of widget." This is about standing out. There are a lot of different places that carry a lot of different products. You want to stand out in your customer's mind for what you do really well.
- "Satisfaction guaranteed." Sadly, this no longer means as much as it used to.
- And others like "We are the best _____ in town."

All customers hear when you use things like that is "blah blah blah blah blah." It doesn't really mean anything to the customer.

Overall Business USP's That Sell

Let's take a look at some examples of industries that have USPs that sell:
- Fed-Ex: "When it absolutely, positively has to be there next day." When you have a high priority document that you need to get somewhere overnight, you choose FedEx.
- Raymour & Flanigan: "3-Day delivery guaranteed." They have guaranteed delivery of your furniture in 3-days or less. They were the first furniture retailer in New England to offer 3-day delivery, so if you need it fast, you choose Raymour & Flanigan.
- Domino's: "Delivery in 30 minutes or its free." If you are hungry and need pizza fast, then you choose Domino's.

So what do all those USP's have in common? They were all in high competition industries and business. They spoke to their target market with their USPs. Most target a niche within a niche. Not everyone wants fast pizzas; some people want pizza that tastes delicious. Not everyone wants furniture in 3 days; some people want custom furniture. So, they spoke to their market places. It was usually a niche within a niche.

All were regular, boring products like furniture, mail delivery, and pizza. There was nothing special about the industries on the examples I just gave you. They were things that you could use right away. They were precise enough to echo the prospects' thoughts. So if you're sitting at home and you wanted something to eat quickly without cooking, you choose Domino's. They were guaranteeing either it's 30 minutes or it's free. It echoed in your thoughts, so you then set your clock, and it became a game.

USP's work because they address the biggest objection or fear to buying. If you were in the market for furniture and you came across Raymour & Flanigan's ads, you definitely paid attention. After all, there's nothing worse than paying thousands of dollars for furniture and having to wait six months when you wanted it in 3 days or less.

They also promise to solve one problem that the prospect will pay to have solved. If you wanted something overnight and you were willing to pay that premium to Fed-Ex to get it there overnight, that wasn't a big problem.

It includes the dominant emotion driving the prospect. You want it fast, and you need it quick—dominant emotions.

It's unique enough to be easily memorable. Most business owners don't have the guts to make strong guarantees. It's just what it is. But if Fed-Ex did it... if Domino's did it... if Raymour & Flanigan did it, you can do it too!

You just have to be creative, and you have to take the time to make sure that you can deliver on your promise. Yet, it's a worthwhile investment.

Chapter 7

Google My Business

Google My Business is an invaluable tool for any business owner who wants people to know where they are located and wants to be near the top of the page one of Google. Understanding the fundamentals of this platform will increase your chances of being found in local and mobile search results.

As a small business looking to connect with more local searchers, these search results are the most valuable ones you can pursue. Getting ranked locally is also a lot easier and less time consuming than attempting to compete with the entire world. Not only that, but focusing on local rankings will also help you reach geo-targeted consumers who are more likely to become real customers.

Google My Business is a new dashboard which replaces Google Places for Business and Google+ Local. Google has experimented with both platforms in the past, which has left many business owners feeling confused and frustrated.

The new Google My Business dashboard will eliminate this confusion by allowing you to manage your company information across all of Google's platforms, including Search, Maps, and Google+. It's a one-stop solution that should help you simplify the whole listing management process in the going forward.

Accessing the dashboard is easy. You can do it from the Google My Business platform on your PC, or you can download the Google My Business App for the Android iOS and use it on your mobile device. Either method will allow you to access and control all of the dashboard functions.

While I can't promise you that Google won't change things up in the future, I can promise that this integrated system makes things a lot easier right now. So here are some step-by-step instructions to help you become familiar with the Google My Business platform:

1. First, visit the following link: http://www.google.com/business.

2. If you already have a Google Places or Google+ Local account, just sign in. Your listing should have automatically been upgraded to Google My Business. You'll be taken to the new dashboard, which I'll show you in a moment (see Step 6).

3. If you've never done anything with Google before, then you'll need to choose the "Get on Google" button. You'll be taken to the next screen. Simply search for your business name and address; there is a good chance that Google will already have your company listed. That is because they have aggregated information from a lot of different sources to populate their platform. However, there is no guarantee that the information is correct. So this is why you need to complete your profile, verify it, and optimize it.

4. If your business is already in the system you can click on the listing to claim it. Obviously, Google doesn't want just anyone claiming listings; so you will have to verify that you're the rightful owner of the business. Google will either offer you the option to do this right away, over the phone, or they'll want to send a post card with a special code. You won't be able to access all of the features until you complete this verification process.

5. If your business is not in the system, you'll have to add it. Just click on the option that says, "None of these match, add my business." You'll be taken to this very simple form.

Fill out your information. Make sure that you are 100% accurate as you do so. You'll want to use your legal name, your local physical address, and your exact business phone number. All of this information should be entered the exact same way everywhere online, including your website and other local listing sites. For instance, if you routinely type out the word "Street" then make sure you do so here and everywhere else. Don't use "St." If you're ABC Business, LLC., then include the LLC. All of this will matter when it's time to build up your rankings later.

6. Once you've logged in, you'll be able to view your dashboard. You can access all of the Google My Business features. As you can see, you can easily access reviews, insights about your page's performance, the Google Adwords Express feature, the Google+ social media platform and YouTube by interacting with this menu.

FEATURES

Google My Business offers several new and existing features which new users, as well as veteran users of Google Places or Google+ Local, should be aware of. Once you login to the new dashboard, you can take a closer look at how each of these features work together to boost your overall online presence and help you save time.

Pages Type
No small business is the same, so Google gives you some choices when it comes to setting up your local page, based on your business type or industry. You can choose between the Store Front, The Service Area, and the Brand page.

If you already had Google+ Local set up then you should have already been upgraded to the appropriate page type. You can change it by editing your business information.

Virtual Tours
This feature lets you add video so that you can give customers a view of your business in action. Using this feature is a great way to reach out and connect with potential customers. Once people get a behind the scenes

sneak peek into your company, many of them will trust you more and feel more comfortable doing business with you.

Reviews

When you publish solicted reviews on your ProView, that information is now broadcast to Yahoo/Bing for inclusion as a star-rating.

Google My Business makes it much easier to deal with customer reviews. As you may know from previous experience with Google+ Local, reviews play a major role in your ability to rank in Google's local search results.

Reviews also matter to your reputation. It's hard to get someone to try a business if it has a steady stream of bad reviews. So it pays to encourage your customers to leave reviews and for you to engage and respond to reviews (both negative and positive).

Wish a bad review could go away? You can't remove reviews; only Google can do that, which is highly unlikely under normal circumstances. But you can respond to them. From your Dashboard, click "Manage Reviews." You can respond to each review by choosing the "View and Reply" button. This is a very good idea, since it shows people that you actually care about customer service, and that you're willing to engage.

You can thank people for their good reviews, and you can try to work things out with those who have taken the time to leave complaints. Either way, it's far easier than the old process, which involved many more steps.

Review analytics is an incredibly beneficial tool, as it helps you monitor your reputation, not just on Google, but all over the web. It tells you where all of your reviews are coming from, so that you can check them out and respond to them as necessary on other sites.

There's a good chance that Google is using the sum total of all of this review data to make decisions about how it will rank you. In the past, it looked like reviews on other sites had a very small impact on your local rankings. However, this report indicates that reviews on other sites might start playing a larger role in the algorithm. In the meantime, gathering reviews continues to be an important part of the small business owner's marketing strategy. So I would recommend that most business owners focus on getting customers to write the bulk of those reviews into Google My Business.

Insights

The Insights feature allows you to access analytics reports and data so that you can understand how your Google My Business profile is performing. You can view the number of views your pages are getting, the number of times people are clicking through to your primary website, and the number of times people ask for driving directions to your establishment.

You can also view engagement on each of your social posts. If a post is performing particularly well, you'll know that you should use more content like that to drive additional engagements. If a post is performing poorly, you can adjust your social strategy appropriately.

Finally, you can get some insight on your Google+ followers. As you gather followers, Google will attempt to gather data on where those people are coming from, and who they are. If you aren't getting many followers, this data may not show up. But if you are getting many followers, you should see their location, gender, and age. This data can help you plan more audience-appropriate content for your Google+ profile and other marketing efforts.

AdWords Express

If you use pay-per-click (PPC) campaigns to drive traffic to your business website then you'll really enjoy this more user-friendly AdWords interface. Before Google My Business you would have had to go to a separate login page to access AdWords.

Now you can create, launch, activate, and deactivate ads in the same place that you are managing the rest of your Google marketing efforts. You can easily track your ad performance from the AdWords dashboard, as well.

From here, you can make some decisions—are you getting a large enough return on your investment? Do you need to deactivate some campaigns? All of this can be done from the drop down arrow next to the ad name. This will give you a menu that includes options for changing your ad's headline or editing the text, deactivating the ad, or removing it entirely.

Engage and Interact with Google+ Followers
You'll find that this feature functions pretty much as it always did. You'll see a quick social update feature right under your dashboard header. You can simply type and share. However, you will have to get off of your dashboard if you want to interact with the greater social platform. To do this, you will select the Google+ icon on your menu.

By the way, if you haven't been using the Google+ social profile, you should really consider it. Google+ offers a distinct advantage over every other social profile out there because Google includes the content of your posts in the search results. This offers yet another way to get your business seen and heard in an increasingly crowded marketplace. Google+ has become just as important to the average business owner as Facebook, so don't neglect it.

Bulk Upload Tool
There is one more tool I want to share with you. This one isn't as readily apparent on your dashboard as the others.

The Bulk Upload Tool allows a business to easily manage information for ten or more locations. The early Google+ Local platform did not provide business owners with multiple locations any easy or intuitive way to manage these locations. Google My Business has corrected this problem.

Visit **www.searchyourcompany.com** to begin using this tool. You will enter each location's information into an Excel spreadsheet using this template. Then you will upload your spreadsheet. Make sure you read through all of Google's quality guidelines before attempting to do this or you may experience verification problems.

Tips for Using Google My Business

Google can be a bit picky at times. If you want to use Google My Business successfully, then you'll need to employ several best practices to get the most out of the platform. Each of these pointers will help you avoid verification issues, Google penalties, and ranking problems that can prevent you from experiencing all of the benefits Google My Business has to offer.

1. Make sure you complete every step of the process as thoroughly and as completely as possible. Fill out as much information about your business as possible. There a lot of "fake businesses" out there who attempt to set up profiles for nefarious purposes. Google wants to make sure you aren't one of them. If you provide more information you'll give Google more reason to believe your profile is trustworthy, which means you can expect to experience an increase in your rankings.

2. Use your legal business name—not a nickname. Using a nickname or an abbreviated version of your name slows down the verification process, reduces your trustworthiness in Google's eyes, and creates a listing which contradicts listings in other directories—which are important. In a moment, I'll explain exactly why this is so important (see Tip #7).

3. Use your physical, business address precisely as the US Postal Service uses it, right down to spelling out the word "Street" if that is what the postal service does. Again, see Tip #7 to find out why.

4. Use a local phone number—not a 1-800 number. You want to strengthen Google's perception of your business as being a good fit for location based search results. That means you want to show Google an area code that fits the location you're trying to rank for. For a local feel, 800 numbers have become far less trustworthy than traditional local numbers.

5. Add your hours of operation. Again, Google wants to see more information. So do customers. Besides, when you do this you get a perk. Customers who click on your business listing during your hours of operation will see a cheerful, "Open now!" right under your business hours. This may inspire them to take the next step, which is, of course, getting into their truck and showing up at your doorstep.

6. Create a detailed overview of your business. Keep in mind that Google does not want to see slogans, URLs, store codes or phone numbers in this section. You need to avoid exaggerated claims like: "The best mechanical contractor in town!" You can, however, give more details about your location: "A licensed and bonded electrician in Atlanta's Peachtree District" would be just fine.

7. Get NAP (name, address, phone number) citations to improve your rank. You receive a citation when anyone lists your name, address, and phone number somewhere on the Internet. You'll usually see citations in a directory of some kind, but they don't have to be. Placing your NAP in the footer of all of your web pages counts, too. Here's the catch: the NAP has to match the address in Google My Business in order to count. And it has to be an exact match. That's why you're safest using your legal name, and it's why you should take the time to look up the US Postal

Service's version of your address. That's the address that Google is going to treat as trustworthy.

You probably have some citations already thanks to data aggregators. However, you do not have to rely on those services, and, indeed, you shouldn't. You'll miss vital opportunities if you wait for others to list you—and there's no guarantee that others will list your business in an accurate, helpful way.

You should actively make citation-building a priority. You can start by targeting the "usual suspects," which are:

- theBlueBook.com
- Yelp
- Yellowpages.com
- Citysearch.com
- Facebook.com
- Manta.com
- Merchantcircle.com
- Superpages.com
- Switchboard.com

The Whitespark Local Citation Finder is one of the easiest and best tools that you can use in order to update, claim, verify, and add citations across the Internet. You can use it to check and claim existing citations, and you can use it to create new ones. It's incredibly comprehensive. It also allows you to check out your competition, giving you an opportunity to build more citations.

It is a paid tool, but it's not an expensive paid tool. It's also the tool that the pros use to make sure they're hitting every citation opportunity.

Citation building can be tedious. Every site has its own rules and its own verification processes. You'll have to make an account on each site. However, it's also an easy way to market your business. Most web searchers click on the top local search result first. As a result, most of those web searchers end up doing business with that business. Therefore, being first is going to pay off in a big way, so your goal should be to get there (or very close to it at the least).

8. Kill duplicates. You'll want to find any duplicate Google My Business Pages and get rid of them. You'll also want to kill duplicates in every other directory you find as well.

9. Encourage your customers to leave reviews on your listing. Reviews are the other major ranking factor that Google My Business uses to rank your listing. Just make sure you're not offering customers incentives to do so, like discounts or free product. Usually, simply asking or reminding them is enough.

10. Use the photos and virtual tours features whenever possible. With visual content like this, prospects will be able to get a better idea of the types of projects you handle. Plus, Google is more likely to display visual content next to your business listing in the search results. This is great, because visual content is so much more engaging and eye-catching than text alone.

Keeping up with all of Google's changes can be confusing, even for professionals who eat, breathe, and sleep Google every single day. It can be downright frustrating for business owners who also have other products or services to worry about.

Don't feel bad if you are one of the many business owners who just doesn't have the time, energy, or interest to keep up with Google My Business (or whatever Google comes up with next).

I'll be more than happy to work with you, and to help you gather up more leads and more sales through the power of local search marketing. Contact me at: **www.searchyourcompany.com.**

Chapter 8

(If) You've Got To Have a Website, Make It a Power Website

It's all about using your internet presence to grow your business. In this chapter you will discover how to dominate your competitors and own your target market using only the internet and free or paid online tools. A contractor can leverage their website, ProView and the other methods covered herein to create a substantive online footprint to present the best overview view of their company to entice prospects and engage clients.

A savvy business owner can begin to dominate their target market with just a simple website, free Twitter account, free YouTube account and a free Facebook page. The Internet has leveled the playing field and opened up the door for the business owner with a small marketing budget to compete for a large market share. Never before has life-changing success for your business been so easily accessible.

However, the true power isn't simply because a business has a website or social media accounts on the Internet. It's about using your website, social media and various other internet tools (e.g., ProView) to get people to trust your business.

Online Marketing Myths

Although marketing online can dramatically change your business, some business owners believe several myths about marketing online that are simply not true:

1. **Myth #1:** They believe that marketing online is too complicated and expensive for business owners to do.
2. **Myth #2:** If your website is on the first page of Google, then your

business will be flooded with customers.

3. **Myth #3:** All you need is a website, and you are guaranteed to instantly get tons of people to buy from your business. Nothing can be further from the truth.

4. **Myth #4:** That you need to spend a fortune on a very expensive website to get people to visit your website and business.

5. **Myth #5:** Marketing on the internet can solve all your advertising and marketing problems – of course, this is untrue.

6. **Myth #6:** All you need is a Facebook page and a twitter account, and you'll automatically get more customers. Gimme a break.

These myths are holding many business owners back from truly succeeding in their businesses by using the power of the internet. However, even when business owners attempt to market their business online, many still fail. Here are the major reasons why 99% of business owners fail:

- They don't focus on the leads and prospects in their local market - also known as local search.
- They don't have a major strategy to guide their actions. They just have a random set of marketing actions with no plan.
- They don't understand how to create online marketing campaigns that drive people to their business.
- They don't tie their internet marketing actions and strategies with their traditional successful business strategy systems.
- They don't track results, so there's no way to know what is and isn't working.
- They fail to *consistently* market. One-and-done campaigns are not successful in growing businesses.

So stop ignoring the truth. In order to be successful with your online marketing efforts, you need to accept the truth about marketing your business online. People love to talk about their experience at your business. So, that means that people are now using social media sites like Facebook and Twitter and review sites like Urban-spoon and Yelp to share their opinions of your business online. Which means that your potential customers are also using these or similar places to see what other people are saying about you. You would have to be crazy to ignore these trends. As a contractor, Yelp and other consumer sites don't apply, but I'm sure you get the point: you need to monitor your business reputation. You never know where people may be discussing your business online.

That's why it's important that you first setup, monitor and maintain your website, social media webpages and review websites. At the end of the day, what others say about your business, whether good or bad, has a big impact on whether potential customers will give your business a shot.

However, if you don't update, monitor or maintain your online reputation and resources, you're risking losing potential customers. Plus, it's also important for you to have a good grasp of online marketing so that you can track and monitor the results of your online marketing strategies.

Keep in mind that as an independent business owner, you are in a dogfight for customers when you market online because the big boys are many times more likely to provide all of the online things that your customers want.

That's why you must have a game plan for turning tweets, posts and reviews into opportunities. You can't simply throw some stuff up and think it will work. You have to understand the target audience and customers in your market.

Most business owners want a website and a Facebook page so that they can become a big brand and be famous. Well, maybe not. But, it does take more than just a Facebook page and a few tweets here and there to get more business. Growth is only possible if you take the time to create a good plan to market your business *consistently* online in your local area.

It's been tested and proven that localized online and mobile ads are perceived by consumers as more relevant and drive more responses. In fact, local-based marketing strategies make a huge difference in online and mobile ad response. In recent studies, when people were asked what variables or factors would cause them to respond to ads, mobile users said the following:

- Ads that are locally relevant to them by smartphones 73% and tablet 70%
- Ads that offer coupons and promotions by smartphones 72% and tablet 69%
- Ads from known brands: 59% on tablets and 65% on smartphones

The study also found that 66 % of mobile device owners noticed ads, while 33% clicked on mobile ads. So you need to have an online presence and a good overall marketing strategy.

The Mobile Advantage
More importantly than just opening and clicking on ads, people who are searching for a local business with their smart phones and tablets are searching in order to make a quick decision. According to a recent study, 64% of smartphone and 44% of tablet users searching for businesses make a decision within an hour to 24 hours of doing their research. If you think it through, it makes perfect sense. People who are searching on their phones and tablets are most likely on the go. So, if you don't have a well-thought-out online presence and marketing strategy, you're missing out on a steady stream of customers who are ready to make a

decision within an hour or 24 hours of doing searches online. With this information, you simply can't ignore the value of mobile advantage.

The next thing to note is that 70 percent of total time spent with business content on mobile devices took place in apps. In other words, people are spending much more time looking for business options on mobile applications:

- 81% of consumers surveyed have searched for a business on a mobile app in the last 6 months.
- 92% of those surveyed have searched for a business on the web in the last 6 months.
- 75% of consumers surveyed often choose a business based on search results of when they searched.
- And 84% of consumers look at more than one business before choosing where they want to shop.

Studies have also shown that three out of five people who are searching for a business on a mobile device don't have a specific business in mind when they start their search. In other words, they're searching for answers. The main criteria that impacted what business consumers chose was the following:

- Location or proximity — so 65% of Smartphone Users and 52% of Tablet Users were focused on location or proximity to where they were searching from.
- The Price — about 48% of Smartphone Users and about the same amount of Tablet Users were focused on price.
- Then 27% of smartphone users versus 43% of tablet users were focused on the good reviews that were online about the business or potential location they were going to.

Obviously, in a business-to-business marketing scenario as-in contracting, it is a bit different. However, every B2B contact is also a consumer and the behavior is similar. From this you can infer that mobile strategies are crucial.

Just another Tool

Many business owners get stressed out over how rapidly the Internet changes and how they can best use it to promote their business. The first thing you need to keep in mind about using the Internet to grow your business sales is that the Internet is just a tool for you to use in your business marketing toolbox. Don't get overwhelmed by all the options and new websites, software and programs that are coming out every day. You must have a simple plan that you create once, review each week and update constantly and execute it persistently.

The ideal plan for generating customers from the Internet doesn't have to be complicated. However, you must follow a specific set of steps in order to do it successfully, such as:

1. **You need to map out your process** – This includes mapping out your entire process for working with a prospect generated from any source on the internet.
2. **You need to identify your target prospect** - In order for any marketing or business growth strategy to work, you have to first know who you're trying to get or who you are trying to attract to your business
3. **You need to create your offer-** Once you attract prospects to your website or social media webpage, you need to have one or more compelling and persuasive offers to get them into your business quickly.
4. **Attracting the prospects** - This is all about selecting online marketing strategies that gets your offer in front of your target prospects.
5. **Lead Capture** – This is your method for getting prospects to give

you their contact information in exchange for the offer or good that they are going to get.

6. **Cultivating Your Leads** – These are your tactics for building a relationship with your database of contacts over time in order to make your offer and then get them into your business quickly.

Following this proven blueprint eliminates the guesswork, confusion and dramatically eliminates the risk of major failure of your marketing efforts. You will grow to love following up with the leads that are generated from your online marketing efforts because you have a proven blueprint to convert them into paying customers. More importantly, your customers will enjoy coming to your business and will become raving fans.

If you need help designing or implementing a strategic marketing plan, reach out to me at **www.searchyourcompany.com.**

Chapter 9

LinkedIn:

Where Businesses Go To Meet Businesses

People are re-discovering LinkedIn®, so you may find you need to re-visit this professional social platform too, since it's a safe bet this group includes your current and potential clients. As Facebook grows ever more disjointed in what it arbitrarily chooses to share, employers, clients and B2B service seekers are turning back to LinkedIn® in a search for reliable connections and information.

LinkedIn® has worked hard to make its platform more user-friendly. It seems to have taken note of and adapted to current-day communication preferences and trends.

It also seems to have recognized the importance of allowing you to present yourself and your brand more like a dynamic, interactive presentation and less like an old-fashioned résumé. And this powerful professional networking platform is presenting more and more useful options regularly.

The best way to experience the power of what LinkedIn® can do is to see how top business figures are effectively using it. LinkedIn® has strict privacy policies, so you won't see identifiable screenshots from within that platform, but let's take a quick look at what top influencers are saying and sharing in their own words...

Step One: Re-visit your LinkedIn® Profile

Is your LinkedIn® **public profile** current? Have you tweaked it to maximum effectiveness for attracting potential clients and leads?

You followed the set up wizard, but possibly skipped certain steps (an option with LinkedIn® setup). Re-visiting this may be "un-sexy"—but vital to core success.

Even if you filled out every bit of information and skipped no steps, take the time to read through the following recommendations and make sure you have included these four specific basics that will directly affect your SEO:

1. **Make sure your Public profile is "visible to everyone"**
Just select the correct radio button on the right side of your screen.

2. **Create your unique vanity URL**
It's a fact. People will search for you on LinkedIn® by guessing at your LinkedIn® URL. Help them achieve the satisfaction of being shrewd guessers by setting up a simple URL that can easily be remembered (and makes you look more professionally important).

It will take you less than a minute. Just go to your LinkedIn® settings and <u>edit your URL</u>. (Lower right-hand sidebar.) Do this and instead of a bunch of numbers after "http://linkedin.com/in/" put your name instead, like so:
   - "http://www.linkedin.com/in/petersmith"

When someone views your profile, your personal, unique LinkedIn® URL will display twice at the top of their browser:

3. **Create a LinkedIn® profile badge to display on your website**
It's the work of literally one click to create a professional-looking LinkedIn® badge (button) to display on your website. Underneath the instructions for changing your URL, you'll see the anchor text: "Create a public profile badge."

Click on this link. You will instantly see a variety of badges in multiple sizes and shapes, together with your personal HTML code snippets in a text box.

Copy-paste your preferred text snippet into the correct spot on your website (or into a sidebar widget, if you are using WordPress and prefer your badges in a sidebar).

4. **You might be shy, but use a Profile Photo!**
   And of course, make sure that when people search for you, they see an attractive, friendly but professional, head-and-shoulders profile photo. (You'd think this would be too simple to mention, but it is amazing, whenever you look through people to add, how many of your peers you will still find with the dreaded "Blank Headshot".)

   Leave your headshot blank and all your other optimization and time spent on your LinkedIn® profile will be wasted. Why would anyone want to go check out a blank profile when it's obvious the person posting it doesn't care?

These are essential basics that people sometimes skip—and *forget to update*. If that applies to you, go complete these actions now. They are crucial to your LinkedIn® searchability and what we will call "openability". They help increase that crucial first impression.

But there's more to tweaking your profile than just the basics we've just reviewed.

You don't just want to "tweak": You want to grab perfectly-targeted leads—the specific type of person you want your business profile to attract.

So before you revise anything, you need to stop and invest time in the following action:

- **Decide on your main LinkedIn® goal.**
  You do want to reach more clients. But who exactly *are* you planning to attract via LinkedIn®? What do you want them to notice? What do you want them to do?

- o What do you want your profile to do for you?
- o What do they need to know about you?
- o What do you want it to say?
- o Why is this relevant to the reason for their searches?
- o Who do you want them to see?

Simply listing your achievements and awards no longer cuts it, unless you are actually job-hunting and presenting a résumé. You need to show yourself in the best light as *the exact go-to expert your potential clients are searching for*.

We will come back to power-charging your profile, but first it's important to understand making the most of LinkedIn® connections before we make any more decisions on how to upgrade your profile further.

Step Two: Connecting with the Right People

Your LinkedIn® network connections are like treasure in the bank, so treat them as such. On this network more than any other, you don't want to add people whose profiles bear no relevance to your main business goal—that's like hosting a vegetarian dinner party and serving only meat. Imagine the effect on those sitting down to such a dinner!

So be ruthless, and use this network only for connections who are totally relevant not just to your goal, but to your other connections as well. Not only will your "guests" be sitting down to a perfectly chosen feast, they'll be surrounded by scintillating (and prominent) company—including you!

The easiest way to start is with the suggestions in the right-hand sidebar, when you are on your LinkedIn® home page, under "People You May Know." Now most of the people suggested you will either not know from a hole in the wall or know really well but have long ago decided not to add. Don't dismiss them so easily! Click on the "See more" anchor text at the bottom of the small selection group. A new page will open up, displaying many choices for you to connect with.

Decide before searching who you want to connect with—and why. Even if you only want to connect with prospective clients, remember that adding peers in related professions and connecting with experts and role models can also help introduce you, via each other's connections that become available, to more prospective clients.

DO NOT click on "Connect"—no matter how well you know the prospective connection! This will instantly send an automated, impersonal invitation to connect—a complete "no-no" on LinkedIn®.

Instead, click on the person's ***name***. This will open up their profile and you can (a) view it fully (b) connect with them through the usual form letter that you can then personalize.

In addition to potential clients, one of the best ways to clarify your own profile needs is to look at how LinkedIn® top movers are doing this. We can't take screen shots of their actual profiles—LinkedIn® privacy rules prohibit this—but you can search for top figures in your field and view their public profiles for yourself.

If you know the name of a specific person to search for, finding the top people is easy. But you also want to check out more than just the people you know.

1. **Start with Alumni**
   Click on "Connections" and choose "Find Alumni" from the drop-down menu.

   You will be prompted to enter your university or other educational institution that you attended.

2. **Explore different categories**

    But notice it also prompts you to "Search universities" directly in the Search bar. This is faster than filling in your information, and you can search institutions you didn't actually attend.

    Click on the little drop-down arrow to the left of the search bar, and there are other suggestions you can choose from:

    - All
    - People
    - Jobs
    - Companies
    - Groups (LinkedIn®)
    - Posts (LinkedIn®)
    - Inbox (LinkedIn®)

    For example, type in any company name (such as "Google") and you'll immediately see not only the company itself and any subsidiary, but also:

    ○ People who work at *[company name]*
    ○ People who used to work at *[company name]*

    You can then use this to check out profiles of key executives. (Pay particular attention to those in the 500+ LinkedIn® category.)

    What type of information do they feature first about themselves? What do their profiles say that particularly catches your attention? What do they include that excites you? Makes you want to click through?

    What do they include that bores you to death?

    Check out twenty top professionals in your field and make

notes (or take screenshots—for your own personal reference only, of course) as aids in helping you compose your own dynamite profile summary.

Searching through Groups can be particularly invaluable—in finding not just Groups, but also potential clients and top experts to study and follow.

For example, studying coaches can be particularly helpful (just type the word "coach" in the search bar for suggestions). You'll find many coaches have that prized "500+ Connections" notation in the bottom-right corner of their profile header bar.

Rinse-and-repeat with other Search categories, too.

As you view the profiles of potential connections (both potential clients and experts you need to study or follow) you will see many different types of approaches, including who prefers to lead off in their opening line or paragraph with:

- A summation of their mission statement or philosophy
- A statement demonstrating he or she knows what is "important to you" (i.e. the person reading the profile)
- A summation of what that professional loves about her job and why she does it
- Instantly telling you what her job is (e.g. "highly organized project coordinator who...")
- "Who I am"
- What they do and how they do it.
- What he or she can help you to do/achieve
- Short summaries

You may also have felt annoyed or frustrated during your search when you came across someone who keeps their profile "Private", forcing you to "upgrade" to view it.

If you want someone to find you, is this really a good idea? Or do you find it necessary to keep the riff-raff from annoying you with too many inappropriate connection requests? (Something to consider when setting your own privacy options).

3. **Use LinkedIn® Advanced Search to Find Potential Leads**
   In addition to using the drop-down on the left side of your Search bar, also select "Advanced" on the right. This will allow you to make your search even more specific.

   Remember to keep connections aligned with your LinkedIn® goal and purpose. This is not Facebook—you can really hurt yourself professionally by connecting with the wrong people (or at least seriously dilute the power of your profile).

   It's not about numbers—it's about relevance.

Step Three: Apply What You've Studied to your Own Lead-Grabbing Profile

Now that you've strengthened your connection base with new, highly relevant contacts and studied what top professionals and LinkedIn® "stars" are doing right, it's time to revisit (a.k.a. continue editing) your own profile and apply the best of what you've learned:

- **Drop** mind-numbing, repetitive or redundant, weak phrases such as "My professional experience includes..." Start out with an active statement: "Highly organized project coordinator" is going to grab the attention of someone looking for a project coordinator much more than "my professional experience includes" and a list of tasks (most likely not even organized in list form, but buried in long paragraphs).

- **Avoid** clichéd phrases such as "a vast array" or "people person." This is all old-style, résumé-type, corporate babble, and does nothing to convince potential clients you are a dynamic power-house who has what they need!
- **Include** your best keywords in your job description, tagline and summary first sentence. These are not only what will help you be found in searches, but what will catch your ideal prospect's eye when he or she does reach your profile!

__What is out__: Writing summaries in the third person.

__What is in__: Keeping it short. Writing summaries in the first person. Being creative and innovative. Making sure you have a unique, strong voice.

Remember, your profile summary's main job is not to fill people in on your life history; it is to help them decide if *you are the perfect person.*

Keep your Summaries and Specialties separate either by actually making sure they are displayed in separate Summary and Specialties category slugs, or by using **sub-heads** to break information down into separate sections.

Step Four: Generating Client Opportunities on LinkedIn®

One of the best ways to generate client opportunities is to let people know that landing clients is your main focus.

There are proven ways to achieve that. You can pick and choose from these suggestions, since not all may be suitable for your business needs:

1. **Start Your Profile Summary with your Experience**
   If you are in an industry focused on performance and your

portfolio (e.g. graphic design, web coding, technical illustration) it is essential to skip all the touchy-feely.

Go straight for the jugular by moving your experience section to the front of what people will see.

2. **Join Relevant Groups**

This has long been a proven strategy for finding customers and clients; and if anything, has become even more effective.

Find groups where you can help people—ones where your potential clients or customers hang out and discuss the topic you dominate—and quietly blend in. Do your best to fit in naturally, like "one of the gang", rather than thinking of yourself as "an expert." And choose Groups with a specific, not generic, focus.

Here's what works best, in this exact order:
- Introduce yourself
- Listen
- Answer questions
- Listen
- Give feedback
- Listen
- Share resources
- Create resources in response to expressed need
- Make sure your own landing pages that you send people contain prominent calls to action and links to products, services or programs.
(If you've provided the right incentive, the people who end up on these pages will be looking for them! Don't make the fatal mistake of landing them there with no additional paid solutions there for the taking.)

3. **Look for Better Suggested Keywords**

When you are filling in your headline, simply click on "Show examples" to see what your peers are putting in their headers (you'll see examples even if you haven't added any connections yet).

This can trigger ideas for much stronger keywords

4. **Add Different Media Types to your Summary**

   Don't just tell viewers you're a great graphic designer; add portfolio images or a video with highlights from your last art exhibit to your Experience section. If you're a virtual assistant, share a slide show or presentation you created for your own site (or a client's, if you have permission).

   You can add multiple types of media to almost every section of your Summary. What best represents you and your work? What will catch their interest, then knock their socks off?

   Don't tell them what you do—show them!

5. **Use a Custom Background**

   You can now put a custom background (similar to a Facebook Cover Photo) behind your profile photo and information. It's as easy as clicking on the little "i" icon and selecting a photo to upload.

   Although LinkedIn® suggests 1,400 X 425 pixels as the preferred size, this figure is somewhat flexible and you can drag to reposition.

6. **Ask to be Recommended**

   When you access your Profile, you will see a small down arrow beside the "Edit your Profile" button. Click on it and survey the additional connection options it presents.

   If you have existing happy clients who you have connected with via LinkedIn®, do check off "Ask to be recommended."

   On the page that opens up, note that you can also choose to give recommendations. Used selectively, making sure you recommend peers for their top skills (and that you have first-hand experience with them in this capacity), this can create goodwill and reciprocity. Solidifying your professional relationships makes you look good to potential clients.

7. **Share your LinkedIn® Profile**

   Put that badge on your website. Add it to your relevant Facebook Page(s). Share when you update it with significant content (otherwise keep update notifications OFF when editing your profile: Turn them on again when you have something really important to share).

   And keep in mind you can share your Profile via .PDF, too.

8. **Check your Network Updates**

   To ensure you are on top of current developments and check on your interaction, visit your home page daily. In the right hand column you can see information such as:

   - Who has viewed your profile in the last 90 days
   - People you may know
   - Ads that may be of interest
   - Posts and updates that may prove useful

   And remember to check out LinkedIn® Pulse, their new channel—this is where you get to select top industry influencers to follow.

Explore all LinkedIn's features and join a LinkedIn-centred Group such as "LinkedIn for Journalists" "Friends of LinkedIn" "LinkedIn Mobile" as well as other targeted Groups. (Make a commitment to your Groups and check activity regularly!)

Keep your profile updated and fresh, and respond to requests quickly. Share your LinkedIn posts on Twitter regularly, just as you check LinkedIn® every day.

And one more thing: Make sure you adjust your settings by clicking "Select what others see when you've viewed their profile." Then make your name and headline visible by checking the radio button.

Allowing people to see who you are and that you have displayed an interest in them is not normally seen as intrusive. In fact, it can be a good thing that often results in connection requests, especially if your title contains the keywords they like to network with or hire.

LinkedIn® is a dynamic, powerful, professional network. Respect it, use it, and help out people who need your services by tapping into those potent leads!

Chapter 10

Other Social Media:
Circles and Cat Pictures

Managing everything that has to be done for social media marketing can be overwhelming. It's important that you have a way to ensure that you cover all the bases. Each social media marketing platform needs its own individual plan, but this overview checklist can help you identify what you need to create an effective social media marketing plan on any network.

Develop Your Social Media Marketing Strategy

➢ Know Your Audience -- Depending on the particular product you're promoting, your audience might be slightly different. For instance, if you are promoting a membership program you may only be marketing it to those who have purchased your book. Understand exactly who the audience is before you begin.

➢ Study Your Industry & Know the Influencers -- Understanding everything you can about your industry is imperative in making any social media marketing strategy work. Identify key influencers

➢ Identify Your Competition -- Don't let competition frighten you. In fact, if you think you have no competition, it should make you question whether or not you have a viable product or service. Keeping tabs on your competition can only make you better.

➢ Define Social Media Networks / Platforms -- Based on the knowledge you have about your audience, your industry and competition, you should be able to identify particular social media networks and platforms to implement your marketing program.

Identify Your Resources & Budget

➤ Staff -- Do you have people in your organization now who can step up and assist with your social media marketing plan implementation?

➤ Contractors -- Do you know of contractors who can assist in these endeavors? If you don't know any, ask colleagues. Make a list of experts who can help you.

➤ Software -- What type of software might you need to help you with organizing, planning and implementation of your marketing plan?

➤ Dollars -- How much money can you devote to your marketing plan?

➤ Time -- Many people discount the cost of time when making a social media marketing plan. It's important that you count any time you must invest so that you can decide how to find the time to execute the strategy.

Determine How You Will Manage Social Media Marketing

➤ Social Media Management Software -- There are many different types of software available such as HootSuite.com which can make managing social media a breeze.

➤ Virtual & Staff Contractors -- Choose the contractors and / or staff who will be responsible for organizing, planning and implementation of your overall social media marketing plan.

➤ Online Project Management Systems -- Choose a project management system to use to help with implementation. If you already have one, add in social media marketing as a project along with the people who will be responsible for different tasks.

Develop Campaign Goals & Objectives

➤ Offer & Messaging -- Set up your offers and messaging for each social media platform that you choose to work with.

➤ USP -- Focus on your unique selling point to help you separate yourself from the competition.

➢ Calls to Action -- Don't skip the calls to action. Every time you submit a message through social media it needs to have a call to action based on the goal of the message.

➢ Your Point -- Never forget why you're doing this. The point of the whole thing will depend for each campaign, so keep referring back to the point to help you develop your messaging.

Optimize All Content & Marketing Materials

➢ Prepare Marketing Collateral -- Press releases, blog posts, articles, images and more all need to be prepared with each platform and message that you have in mind. You won't always want to share the same image on Pinterest that you do on Facebook without some modifications.

➢ Optimize Content -- Content includes everything mentioned above. Ensure that your titles, the words you use, the benefits you describe, and the pictures you pick relate to your goals, your products, your services and your brand.

Optimize & Improve Online Real Estate

➢ WebPages -- Is your webpage responsive? If not, it's time to ensure that it is. Responsive design is imperative with social media marketing because most people use their Smartphones to access social media.

➢ Blogs -- Can your audience read your blog from any device? Just like it's important to design your website so that everything on there is responsive and works well, the same goes for your blog.

➢ Newsletters -- If you send out a newsletter is it focused, targeted, relevant, and responsive? Does it focus on providing the customer the education they need to make good choices?

➢ Overall Branding -- Be consistent across all social media platforms with your brand, but also change it up for each social network based on that network's personality.

Complete & Customize Your Social Media Profiles

On each platform it's important that you personalize your profile, optimize images and make the social media unique to that particular platform, but still representative of your brand.

> ➤ LinkedIn -- Connect with new people and related companies each week. Try to set a weekly goal. Ask for recommendations of any one you've worked with on a regular basis. Don't use the auto feature and send a mass request, make it more personal and build your profile and network slowly. Update your status daily.

> ➤ YouTube -- Each week subscribe to at least one new channel related to your industry. Look for relevant videos to share on other social networks weekly. Record short tip videos each week to share with your audience. (Tip: Record your Google Hangouts)

Build Your Social Media Networks

> ➤ Connect -- You probably already have people that you can connect with on each social media platform you join. Shoot for about 25 connects/followers/likes etc., to start with and then build on that each week.

> ➤ Engage -- Understand social media etiquette for each network you choose to post on. Be professional, make it about them, and seek to be a resource. The more you make it about them, and building relationships, the better social media will work for your business marketing.

> ➤ Share -- Don't just share your own work, share other people's work that is relevant to your industry and audience. Always remember the audience and ask yourself "Is this relevant to my audience?" If yes, share, if not, don't.

> ➤ Recommend -- It might seem counterintuitive to recommend other businesses, products, and services to your audience but the truth is, sometimes someone else will be better for the job. If you recommend good people, they will return the favor.

- ➢ Build Expertise & Credibility -- Share original content, relevant studies, books, webinars, and more with your audience when related. By adding in your own content and comments about the things you share you will build up your expertise. By sharing only relevant and screened information you build your credibility.

Monitor Your Metrics

- ➢ Engagement Level -- Before starting with metrics you should know your objective and have a way to measure that objective. Using a tool like HootSuite.com can help you measure engagement on a whole new level.
- ➢ Customer Satisfaction -- Are your customer's satisfied once they convert? If you're not sure, try asking them using social media.
- ➢ Calls to Action Effectiveness -- Are your calls to action working and producing the results you expect? If you're getting results but not what you expected, try testing other ideas to see what works best.
- ➢ Feedback -- Always ask for feedback from movers and shakers and experts as well as your contacts, friends, followers, and likes. Let them lead the way and you won't be disappointed in the results.
- ➢ Other -- Any objective that you have should be reflected in a metric that you can monitor. Objectives are always exact and measurable.

Using this checklist to help set up your social media marketing plan can help you remember what's important and avoid missing relevant ideas.

Chapter 11

Your Reputation

What Do Customers Say When You're Not In The Room?

More and more small businesses today are using online directories to their benefit. If you run a small business, odds are you spend a great deal of your time thinking about your marketing plan. Online directories can be a great addition to your current small business marketing strategy. Online directories can help your small business expand its website traffic, increase the likelihood that your website will be found by interested viewers and increase your bottom line. If you haven't taken a look at online directories and considered how your small business could use them to increase its market presence, then now is the time to start!

There are many different types of online directories available on the Internet. Each of these online directories serves a specific purpose and can be used by your small business in specific ways. An online directory is a website that allows your small business's website to be added to a specific category where it can be searched for by interested viewers. These searchable online directories allow their viewers to search for websites and businesses that they find interesting or that they want to learn more about. Listing your small business on an online directory increases your website's visibility on the web and helps to create inbound links to your business's website. Online directories make it easy for people to find what they are looking for. For a contractor, The Blue Book offers a directory that puts you in front of those with projects needing bids. Talk about targeted eyeballs belonging to decision makers!

Every website which is submitted to an online directory is placed in a specific category. These categories can range in how they are organized.

Some are organized by business-related categories, some are organized according to personal preferences and others are organized by subject. Each category consists of several websites relating to a specific topic. Each website listing features the name of the website, a direct link to the website and a short description of the website. Interested internet viewers will be able to browse through the various categories in the directory and locate websites like yours that they may be interested in viewing. Essentially, online directories make it easier for random viewers to find your business's website.

The concept of online directories is actually a pretty simple one. A directory is just a listing place for a number of websites. Any type of website could be listed in an online directory. Some online directories are huge and cover every topic that someone could create a website for, while others are very small and exclusive to a specific niche.

Let's use an example. Say you are a coin enthusiast and you want to find some websites that cater to your specific interest. You could look through a huge online directory such as Yahoo's online website directory and find several dozen websites that are related to coin collecting. Or you could look for an online directory that is niche-specific, which means that the entire online directory would be based on hobbies such as coin collecting. With a niche-specific directory you may find even more websites that are based on your specific interest than what you could find on the larger directories.

Since online directories are organized by categories, finding websites that relate to a specific interest such as coin collecting is very easy. You could find information and websites about coin collecting in your local region, too, if you use a regional-specific online directory. So if you live in Denver, you could find websites that relate to both coin collecting and the Denver area. Online directories will direct you to websites that you want to find. All you have to do is perform a search in the online directory for a specific topic or browse through the various categories until you find the type of websites you are looking for. When you perform a search you will be given a list of all of the websites that relate to your search term. You will be presented with a number of links to these websites and each link will have a short description of what you are likely to find on the website. You can read the descriptions and choose to click on the website that best suits you.

There are many different types of websites that you could find under a specific topic as well. For example, if you search several online directories for information relating to coin collecting you may find websites that are about finding coins, buying coins or selling coins, along with associations that you could join regarding coin collecting. These are just a few of the examples you could find using an online directory. There are simply too many topics to list them all here.

You can see how anyone can use an online directory to find websites relating to things that interest them. As a small business owner you can see how people who could be potential customers of yours are using online directories, too. Now that you understand how online directories work, it is time to see how they can work for your business.

How Do Online Directories Benefit Small Businesses?

There are many benefits associated with listing your small business in an online directory. The more online directories you can use to list your business, the more benefits you will reap. Here are some of the benefits of using online directories:

- **Exposure**
  Exposure is important for all business marketing strategies. After all, the more people who are exposed to your business, the more people are likely to utilize your business's services. If online viewers aren't able to see your website or even know that it

exists, then they probably aren't going to purchase your products or services. Listing your business's website in online directories helps your website to gain exposure. Thousands of people use online directories every day to find things they are interested in. These are people who are actively searching for websites that are directly related to your products or services. They are already looking, so all you have to do is make it easy for them to find you. Online directories will expose your business to more online viewers, which could increase traffic to your website.

- **Increased Traffic**

  There are several ways that online directories can help you increase the amount of traffic your website receives. For starters, the more exposure your website has, the more people are likely to visit it. But online directories offer more than just exposure from potential viewers. They also offer exposure to the various major search engine crawlers like Google and Yahoo. This increases the chances that your website will appear on major search engine results pages or SERPs, which will allow more people to see the website when they perform a regular search. Both search engine optimization exposure and exposure to more people who are searching for your website could result in increased traffic to your small business's website.

- **Affordable Advertising**

  As a small business owner you already understand the importance of advertising. You know that it helps customers to find your business and recognize your name and brand. You probably think you have little room in your budget for more advertising. One of the major benefits of listing your business's website in an online directory is that the directories are specific to geography or industry or both. This specificity provides efficiency on your advertising spend. If you try to market in mass media, you are paying for unqualified eyeballs. Directories offer curated, specific niche oriented prospects. This makes them one of the highest ROI online advertising methods.

- **Professional Appearance**

You want everything about your business to look professional in the eyes of your customers. A professional appearance enhances your status and makes customers more likely to patronize your business. Online directories help you to look like a professional business. When an online consumer sees your business listing in an online directory they will consider your business to be an authority on the subject and a professional place to do business. Unlike a search that is performed on a major search engine like Google, where there is little difference between the legitimate websites relating to a topic and the less than useful websites, online directories are mostly legitimate websites. Online consumers are more likely to trust what they see on online directories.

- **SEO Benefits**

Online directories offer several search engine optimization or SEO, benefits as well. Firstly, these online directories offer you more inbound links. When an online viewer sees your website link in an online directory, they will be able to click on it and be instantly re-directed to your website. This is a great way to increase traffic. It is a great way to improve your status in the eyes of search engine crawlers, too. The more backlinks that a search engine crawler can find, the more relevant they will rank your website. This is especially true of authoritative online directories. Being linked to a major online directory, such as Google Places, will give your website more relevancy in the eyes of Google's search engine crawlers. This will result in a higher page ranking on the SERP. As you know, a higher search engine result page rank you get, the more people are going to click on your website link.

- **Increased Revenue**

  When more people are able to find your website, it increases the chances that they will visit your website. When people visit your website they are more likely to purchase your goods or services. This means that online directories can help you increase your revenue stream. Online directories are good for your bottom line.

- **Increased Brand Recognition and Customer Interaction**

  When an online viewer locates your website though an online directory, they are more likely to remember your business's name and directly interact with it. Online directories can help your business stand out to customers as well. Overall, listing your small business in an online directory will help you to create a more comprehensive and effective online presence.

Listing your small business's website with several online directories will help more people find your website, whether they are specifically searching for it or if they are just browsing around. In addition to gaining exposure, online directories will provide major SEO benefits, which will help your website get found by search engines. Increased exposure and higher search engine rankings will result in more traffic to your website, which will result in higher revenue.

There are many different types of online directories, from large global directories to small, niche and location-specific ones. Some examples of other types of online directories can include reciprocal link directories, free directories, paid directories, Business 2 Business directories, theme-related directories, small business directories and many, many more.

Apart from the concept that online directories will increase the amount of exposure your website gets and help with your SEO strategies, they are also very effective ways to directly target potential customers. Online directories make it easy for online users to find something they want. According to a study performed by Burke, 8 out of 10 people will use a print or online directory to find companies or products they are looking for. The same study also suggested that 8 out of 10 people who use these directories to locate a business do so with the intent to purchase a product or service from them. This is a very effective form of targeted advertising. The customer already needs or wants your product or service and you can directly target them by listing your website in an online directory.

Another reason why you should consider listing your small business has to do with your Return On Investment, or ROI. Since the potential benefits of getting increased website traffic are great compared to how much you will have to spend to list your website in an online directory, you can see a great return on your investment in the form of increased revenue. You also want to keep your brand and your company name in the minds of consumers at all times, which is something else that an online directory can help with.

Even though listing your website in many online directories will improve your website's exposure and SEO ranking, it is not effective to just SPAM your website into every single online directory you can find. You will want to take some time to consider which specific online directories will give you the best ROI. The best option is to find a great combination of directories to join. If you run a small business, the best place to start may be with a local directory. This is because most people will search for businesses in their area they can patronize. Local market and niche-specific online directories can offer extremely targeted advertisements to potential local customers.

After your business is listed in these directories you can take a look at the larger and potentially more expensive general-interest directories. You will probably want to consider listing with the top 10 online directories, as these will be used by a lot of people and will offer higher relevancy and authority in the eyes of search engines. Google Places and Google Maps are large general-interest directories that you will want to list your small business in. If your website sells tangible goods you may also want to consider listing it in comparison shopping websites and product listings directories. Studies show that 42% of consumers will look at a comparison shopping website before they decide to purchase a specific product.

The best way to figure out which specific online directories your small business should be listed in is to start with your competitors. Take a look at your local and niche-specific options and figure out if your competition is already listed. If they are, you need to be listed, too. If they are not listed you may want to list your website as a way to beat them to the punch. In some situations it may not make sense for you to have a listing in a specific online directory, even if your competitors are listed in it. Your goal should be to be listed in every relevant and niche-specific directory you can find, as well as many of the major directories. However, you don't want to be in so many directories that you appear "spammy."

In addition to listing your website in online directories, you also need to maintain these listings. It is important for your online directory listings to be up to date and accurate, or else you could just be wasting your time. If your directory information seems out of date then your customers will undoubtedly look elsewhere.

It will probably take some time to see the results of listing your small business's website in so many online directories, but eventually you will see results. The best way to find the perfect combination of online directory listings for your business is to use some sort of tracking or analytics system. You will want to be able to see how many people clicked on your website links from within the directory and if your website has shown increased traffic since then. You will want to stop wasting your time with online directories that are not producing results and increase the time and effort you spend on online directories that are productive.

Tips For Listing Your Small Business in Online Directories

Now that you understand why your small business should be listed in online directories and have started locating the directories that you want to be listed in, you are ready to begin creating your business listings for submissions. Here are some tips and best practices for listing your small business in online directories:

- Start by choosing local directories and directories that are niche-specific. So if you own a coin shop in Denver, make sure you find a local Denver business directory and a directory that is related to coin collecting. If you can find a coin collecting hobby directory for the Denver area, you are all set.

- Once you're in local directories, start searching for larger and more generalized directories. Pick directories that get a lot of traffic and that are listed highly on major search engines such as Google. A higher search engine ranking means that the directory will be considered as both authoritative and relevant in the eyes of search engines, making any links you get through these directories more valuable to your SEO strategy.

- Include all of the relevant information regarding your small business in your website's directory description. This should include your business's name, location, telephone number, contact information and possibly reviews, business hours and anything else that is relevant. Add in photos, maps or other interactive features if the directory lets you.

- Try to keep your information consistent across all of your online directory listings. This will help your website to retain its credibility in the eyes of search engines and will assist with your SERP rankings.

- Try to make your business stand out by offering an explanation of your business or any specific message the customer should know in your description.
- Keep all of your information up to date. This may mean frequently updating all of your listings several times per month.
- Allow customers to leave positive reviews and use them in your listing if the directory allows it.
- Always be professional and consistent with your business's listings and message. This includes any information regarding your brand.
- If you sell products or services to a local market, make sure your business is listed in a local business directory. Include geo-specific keywords and information. An example would be: "Mike's Coin Collecting" + "Denver."
- Optimize your website for SEO purposes and include the relevant keywords in your meta titles and listing descriptions. Keyword research is important.

Now is also a great time to get your small business listed in the Top 15 Online Directories. There are few other internet marketing techniques that will offer so many benefits for such a small investment on your part. Listing your business in an online directory will increase your website's online presence and help more people find you, which can help you increase your business's revenue.

Chapter 12

Famous In Your Field

When you put your face and your personality in your marketing it makes you stand head and shoulders above your competition because they can't duplicate you. You no longer struggle to find what's unique about your business. Customers or clients have a visible and easily identifiable reason to choose your business, so you can quickly become known as the "go-to expert" for your industry.

And when media does a story on your industry, they are much more likely to go to the perceived expert, regardless if it's true or not.

Most business owners never even consider this strategy because they don't truly believe that they have something unique and valuable to offer their marketplace. Even if you think that you can never be in front of video cameras or be on radio, you can still be the face and personality of your business by writing or compiling resources for your target market.

You can start with something as simple as creating a frequently most asked questions brochure, booklet, video or audio. If you don't truly believe you have anything unique to offer, then you need to take some time away from your business to get your self-worth together because you are valuable and your business is valuable.

Your Secret Weapon

It's always better to be famous in your target market because that's where it matters. See, prospects are magnetically drawn to your business without even knowing why you are famous.

When you implement this strategy it then becomes easy to see how business owners go from struggling and broke to being flush with cash. And you can easily attract too many customers or clients that you can't even handle them all.

And every other marketing strategy you implement is much more effective because it has your name brand on it.

There are dozens of regular business owners who strategically built their companies and brands around themselves instead of a nameless entity. It's a proven formula that you can borrow from.

Notable business owner's who've done this include:
- Anthony Robbins
- Donald Trump
- Oprah Winfrey

Leveraging your persona and expertise allows your customers and clients to connect to you on a deeper level. People are desperate to feel relevant, connected and in the insider's circle. Use that to your advantage.

Putting your personal name and identity on your business implies that you're trustworthy. With deep connections to your clients or customers, you invoke that "Oh yeah, I know him" feeling in your prospects, clients and customers.

The deep connection is how you build loyalty in your clients and customers. It goes beyond filling their needs. It becomes a part of who they are and that's what you want.

However, never try to trick your prospects. You need to spend time on how your business looks so that you're positioned properly in order to attract the ideal type of prospects, clients and customers.

When you are perceived as the obvious expert in your target market, you can charge premium fees. If you needed a surgical operation, would you prefer the hospital with the surgeon who has a book, radio show and local television show with dozens of testimonials or the guy no one has ever heard of? Simple choice, isn't it!

Your mission is to create marketing systems that generate leads AND position you as the obvious go-to expert in your target market. However, underneath the well-polished exterior, there must be a fully functioning and well-oiled business that can actually deliver on every stated and implied promise in your marketing.

There are some types of expertise that customers or clients don't care about. You should focus on only using expertise that benefits your customers or clients like:

- Reports or books you've written to help your ideal prospect choose a specific product or service provider.
- Television, radio or newspaper interviews you've conducted as a consumer advocate or expert in your niche
- Comprehensive case studies or testimonials that clearly show the problem, solutions and benefits your customer's or client's received from hiring or buying from you

But there are some potential downsides of owner persona marketing:

- If you need extended time off, your business could flounder and struggle unless you put the proper systems in place.
- If you no longer want to be the face of your business, it may be difficult for the business to transition to another branding strategy.
- If you ever want to sell your business, you must have marketing systems in place to replace your persona generated leads and sales.
- You must have a personality and demeanor that matches your

target market, otherwise you will cost your business sales revenue and profits.

- It can become a crutch that is used to cover up bad business practices or bad marketing. You must always be able to deliver on the promises you make or imply in your marketing.

Building Your Expertise Overnight!

Use Customer/Client Testimonials In Your Marketing
Trust is a tremendously valuable asset that can take years to build and seconds to destroy. That's why it's so important to gather and collect the solutions and uses for your products or services in the words of your paying customers and clients.

Third party testimonials and case studies add credibility, trust and value to your company that you could likely never produce on your own. You should absolutely coach your customers in how you want your testimonial to be written or created. It allows you to get the maximum value for your efforts.

And ask your customers to leave as much information about themselves as possible to add believability to their testimonials and case studies

Video Marketing
Create video's that inform your prospects and customers while positioning you as a resource and thought leader in your industry. You don't have to be a Hollywood actor to become a local celebrity. You can create great videos for free if you're willing to put in the time to learn how.

The best method is usually hiring an online video expert who can usually create great informative videos ranging in cost depending on what you want to include in your videos.

There is a 99% chance that someone in your niche is already doing video marketing, so simply go to Youtube.com and browse the website using search terms for your industry to get ideas.

And while your videos may never get as many viewers as Jimmy Fallon, Grumpy Cat or seemingly any cat video, you can become the go-to expert for your target market.

Press Release Marketing

The power of using press releases is in your ability to find a unique angle that peaks the interest of local and national media outlets. Because press releases also show up in search engine results, it helps you pass the background checks that customers perform on businesses where they shop.

Your press release can either drive traffic to a specific product or service or be an interesting tie-in with your business. All you need is a good press release writer to scour the media to find a unique angle on a weekly basis to create relevant content.

Don't worry about running out of angles because there are dozens of events that are happening in your local marketplace every day.

Personally Branded Monthly Newsletter

A branded monthly newsletter is your chance to create content and share resources that further prove that you are an expert in your field. You control the content, so you can demonstrate any facet of your expertise that you want. There are no limits to what you can do.

Your monthly newsletter can give your clients an up close and personal look into the person behind the curtain of your business. It's also an excellent way to educate and tweak the interest of your prospects and past clients.

And virtually every business can have some type of a newsletter that will engage the prospects or customers in a meaningful way and on a consistent basis.

Personally Branded Website

Sometimes, it makes sense to also promote yourself as a brand, in addition to and seperately from your business brand. The easiest way to brand your website is to create a series of five to ten videos that introduce you and answer many of your prospects questions, fears and objections to buying from you.

The next best method is to fill your website with content and resources that you've compiled or created. A correctly branded website starts the process of building trust and lubricating the path to making a purchase from you.

Even though your website is personally branded with your face and voice, you should always make your content and sales message about your prospects and what they would want.

The key to having an effectively branded website is to focus on educating your prospect and answering as many of their questions as possible so they can easily make a buying decision.

The Best Investment

A key part of increasing your expertise is investing in your own continuous education and self-development. Without your own constant growth, you will run out of ideas, creativity, knowledge and the ability to stay cutting edge in your business.

So the best investment is the investment you making yourself.

An Open Mind Is A Powerful Thing

Most business owners think that by having a closed mind and staying the course they are showing persistence. Nothing could be further from the truth. See, closed minds don't allow anything to get out, but a closed mind most certainly doesn't welcome new good ideas either. Only by having an open mind can you see many of the opportunities in your business and marketplace. You should examine other successful businesses and ethically steal their best strategies and tactics.

There are hundreds of successful businesses that have solved the very problem you're facing right now. Stop trying to reinvent the wheel.

The Sum Total Of Everything You Do

The actions, habits and standards you execute on a daily basis will ultimately determine the success or failure of your efforts in your business. If you are undisciplined, tough to talk to and rude, then don't be surprised when your employees, customers and distributors reflect the same back to you.

You must do everything in your business as if you're being judged by a panel of your worst critics, because that's exactly what your customers will become if you let the standards start to slide.

Don't Limit Yourself To One Information Source

In order to make an informed decision you need all available information that will allow you to position your business for success. You should own every book, marketing and business-building course that is even remotely related to your business.

You should regularly scour online and offline bookstores for books, videos and reports that cover your industry. You should subscribe to your industry publications and any other publications that are even slightly related to yours. You should actively mystery shop your competition and ask your customers what they think about your competitors.

Find A Mentor, Mastermind Group or Business Coach

In every market and industry there are other business owners who have faced the same challenges as you and have successfully navigated solutions to those very problems. One of your personal missions should be to find a mentor who can walk you through your business challenges and help you find solutions.

Mastermind groups are groups of business professionals who meet regularly to help each other solve their business problems. They are usually from different industries, so they bring a fresh eye and perspective to solving your problems. Marketing is very universal across industries.

A business coach is great for knowing your business intimately and helping you solve very specific problems in uniquely creative ways. So if you have never worked with a business coach before, be prepared to be challenged in a good way. It's a life and business changing decision.

To explore options to get coaching, mentoring or to join a mastermind, reach out to me.

Building Marketing Campaigns Around Your Expertise and Persona

Target The Best Prospects
Every campaign must start with you knowing exactly who your best prospects are. You discover this by examining your past customers and building an ideal customer profile.

You should never build your marketing campaign around the type of customers who complain the most, spend the least and buy the cheapest stuff. By targeting your best prospects, you can focus more of your marketing dollars on the most profitable type of customers. You also can fine-tune your sales process and really optimize your sales funnel when you do this.

Develop A Unique Market Niche
It's next to impossible to be all things to all people, so pick a lucrative niche and focus on dominating that niche. Concentrate on building one complete marketing campaign around your selected niche.

When you focus on one niche, you can channel all of your energy and resources into dominating your niche. It simplifies things for your prospects, customers and staff. And your marketing campaigns become much easier to create and execute.

Position Your Business Correctly

Most business owners are in it for the quick dollar only, so they never even consider positioning as a worthwhile goal. When you choose to become a library of resources that educates your prospect about your products, services and industry, you carve out your own space in the mind of the prospect.

Positioning your business as the best solution can be done by creating marketing resources that educate your prospect or existing customers.

Maintain Your Visibility By Consistently:
➢ Using video marketing as much as possible.
➢ Putting out relevant and timely press releases.
➢ Weaving testimonials into your marketing.
➢ Writing a monthly or quarterly newsletter.
➢ Branding your website with your voice and face.

Maximize your Fame

Find a way to include your third-party credentials in your marketing campaign. Create a credibility showcase package that includes:
• Articles you've had published.
• Projects you've completed.
• Books you've written or contributed to.
• Interviews where you were the person interviewed.
• Newspaper stories or media coverage where your business was featured.
• Informative resources you've created or had created for you.

The Right Place At The Right Time

Place your educational resources all throughout your business so that prospects and customers can see them. If you have a waiting area, place your books, monthly newsletters and brochures there.

You can even play an endless video loop that you've compiled of customer testimonials, interviews and informative tidbits of information. And repurpose all of your content and use it in every facet of your business.

Education Is The Key

Your marketing process of educating your prospects can become your unique sales proposition. At every turn in your business you need to be positioning your company as a resource and a destination for when a prospect is ready to make a decision. Never stop educating your prospect. Not only does it position you for success in your prospect's mind, but it keeps you in the right mindset towards your prospects and customers. Constant education is also necessary for you or your people to keep up with the latest developments in online marketing.

Conclusion

Local Marketing Do's and Don'ts

Do's:

Optimize your website for mobile: Make it easy for customers and followers who use mobile devices, tablets and smartphones. Smartphone and tablet users use their mobile devices two to six times in a week to search local businesses. Google now penalizes sites that are not mobile-optimized.

Assure Accurate Information: You should keep your information accurate and constantly updated and accessible throughout the web and on all publisher's listings. These will increase your search engine ranking.

Offer High Quality Content: Your website content should be impressive and useful for your customers. It will make it easy for your customers to leave reviews about your business. Quality and effective reviews leave a good impression on your customers, while influencing your search engine ranking.

Update your profile: You should update your business profile from time to time with updated images, new product or new services. Search engines love consistently updating information.

Include Media: Videos and Images increase your appeal in your local market by making your offerings more tangible. Search engines love them. Visuals can boost your business rankings and appeal in the market. Contractors can post videos of projects.

You can include customer's testimonials, product demonstrations and customer service staff in your videos and images to make it more powerful.

Correctly Optimize the On Page Signals: On page SEO is associated with page title, URL, header tags, image alt text, and page content. You can consider the geographic area in which you provide service, including suburbs or nearby towns. If you serve several counties, dedicate a page to *each* service area rather than only having one page that says you cover several areas.

You can place keywords, language and content to describe your business and the area with a consistent NAP (name, address and Phone) listing on online directories. This will help local searchers find your business.

Utilize social ambassadors: Social media pages work as a brand ambassador. Some people check their Facebook account more often than their email. You can create mini pages to drive your traffic to your business blog and utilize the social platforms to get more traffic.

Use a Strong call to action: You can include a call to action on your business website. You can run an offer, white paper, free coupons, % off on products, etc. Whatever is appropriate for your business. People always look for offers. With this you can get a great deal of traffic to your website. You can also include this offer information on your landing page.

Claim your Profile: You can list your business in local directories. Each directory serves different purposes, but overall they increase your visibility on the web. Make sure you are only on reputable directories and vigorously manage your business appearing on questionable ones.

You can claim your business on Google Places, Yelp, Manta, Bing Business Portal and others. Power Listings allow you to claim your local business in more than 30+ local search sites in a few minutes.

Stand Out: You should always try to be different and creative to stand out from the crowd in your marketing niche. You should tell your audience what you are providing that your competitors don't. You can give them a reason to purchase from you.

Don'ts:

Don't Create Fake Reviews: Do not write fake reviews for your company. Search engines are getting better at detecting fake reviews, so stay away from that. If you post fake reviews you might face a penalty that can harm your business' local search engine ranking for a long time.

Don't Spam Your Customers: Just because you have the customer's contact information does not mean you should go crazy with your marketing strategies and send them an email every hour. If you do this, your customers will definitely unsubscribe from your lead list forever.

Don't Set it and Forget It: Remember that things change on the web so you have to keep an eye on all the online services you are using for your local marketing. Social Media as well as various online marketing tools are updated often. You must be aware of that for your local online marketing efforts, too.

Don't Use P.O. Box Address: If you use a P.O. Box address for your business then it will be difficult for the search engine to determine where your local business is located geographically. If you run your business in your own home, then you should always use a physical address as your business address (e.g., UPS store).

Don't Focus Only on New Customers: You should appeal to both new and existing customers. New customers are quite interested in your contact information and support, unlike existing customers who are often more interested in your products, discounts and new offers.

Don't Rely Only on Search Engine Traffic: Local people don't always use Google, Bing, Yahoo or other directories to find businesses around their local area. A significant number of local searchers use review sites, portals, applications and other tools to find you.

Don't Over Optimize: Search Engine Optimization is important, but do not try to over-optimize your website. Search engines penalize those who try to game the ranking system to get in the top no matter what. Try to optimize for several keywords at the same time instead of just one.

Don't Use a Toll-Free Number: Using a toll-free telephone number will make it very difficult for the search engines to find your geographical location. Using a land-line phone number will help you avoid this. Besides that, a land-line number will make you look more professional and real.

Don't Pay To Be In Shady Directories: They don't provide any extra benefit to your business. These types of directories are spammy and search engines don't like them. Use high-trust sites like TheBlueBook.com

Don't Ignore Negative Reviews: Negative reviews are a great opportunity to make your product or service even better each time until its perfect. Be kind to people who offer Negative Reviews, thank them for being honest. And tell them you actually use negative feedback to make your product a lot better.

About Jason Myers

Jason Myers is a pilot, inventor, serial entrepreneur, author, and perpetual sponge for knowledge. He has started, invested in and sold many successful offline and online companies since 1991. He is often referred to as a business ninja with a swiss army knife, able to diagnose and fix nearly any issue. Growing businesses with effective marketing is a passion of his.

Jason is Co-founder of CXO Collective International, a Private Equity firm with a non-profit Global Entreprenurial organization that harnesses the triad of Capital, Talent and Opportunities. CXO focuses on Buying, Building and Selling companies. CXO Collective has grown to attract members in 29 U.S. states and 7 countries. Members earn performance based incentives, consulting fees and stock. To learn more, or to join the movement, head on over to **http://www.cxocollective.com/**

You can also contact Jason directly on Linkedin or at:
jason.myers@cxocollective.com

To download the free tools and access more information about the topics in the book, visit: http://www.searchyourcompany.com.

CPSIA information can be obtained at www.ICGtesting.com
Printed in the USA
LVOW10s2349270516

490332LV00002B/3/P